Junior Maths

Book 3

GALORE PARK

Junior Maths

Book 3

David Hillard

Series Editor: Louise Martine

www.galorepark.co.uk

Published by Galore Park Publishing Ltd
19/21 Sayers Lane, Tenterden, Kent TN30 6BW

www.galorepark.co.uk

Layout by Typetechnique
Technical illustrations by Ian Moores
Cartoon illustrations by Gwyneth Williamson
Cover design by The Design Gallery

Printed by Replika Press Pvt. Ltd., India

ISBN: 978 1 905735 26 6

First published 2009, reprinted January 2010, April 2010, 2011, 2012, 2013

To accompany this course:
Junior Maths Book 3 Answer Book ISBN: 978 1 905735 29 7
Junior Maths Book 3 Teacher's Resource D0122090 Available for download from
www.galorepark.co.uk

Details of other Galore Park publications are available at www.galorepark.co.uk

ISEB Revision Guides, publications and examination papers may also be obtained
from Galore Park.

The publishers are grateful for permission to use the photographs as follows:
Page 13 Roger Harris/Science Photo Library; page 27 Mehau Kulyk/Science Photo
Library; page 56 David Mack/Science Photo Library; page 75 Matt Meadows, Peter
Arnold Inc./Science Photo Library; page 173 Dr Keith Wheeler/Science Photo Library;
page 312 Adrian Thomas/Science Photo Library.

About the author

David Hillard has spent more than 45 years teaching Mathematics in two preparatory schools. Generally he has taught those who would not describe themselves as particularly proficient at the subject.

Since 1980 he has been associated with the Common Entrance Examination at 11+, 12+ and 13+ levels in the role of either adviser, assessor or setter. He played a significant part in the revision of the syllabus in 2003 when the present format of the examination was introduced.

He is a co-author of the successful *Fundamental Mathematics* series, first published in 1984.

Preface

Book 3 continues the *Junior Maths* series. The content is aimed at children in Year 5. As with previous volumes, the author aims to provide a sound and varied foundation on which the pupil can build in the future. There is plenty of material to support this but at the same time there are possibilities for the more able to be extended.

The author does not wish to dictate to either pupil or teacher. A combination of approaches, the more modern 'mental' and the more historical 'traditional', are both explored so that the appropriate method for the individual can be adopted.

As before, there is no prescribed teaching order. Topics may well be looked at more than once during the year. The author is convinced that it is the teacher who knows what is best for each individual pupil and when each topic should be introduced.

The full chapter on Mental Strategies is available as a free download from the Galore Park website www.galorepark.co.uk with a short introduction in this book. Mental agility is a helpful weapon in the armoury of those of all ability levels.

Mathematics is so often a question of patterns. Each chapter ends with a free-standing activity, either numerical or spatial, to cover this aspect of the subject.

Acknowledgements

It is the author's name on the book's spine but the production of a book relies on so many different departments dovetailing in unison. It is very much the case that the strength of the whole is the sum of the strengths of the individual parts. I have been extremely fortunate in the backing I have received from the whole team at Galore Park. This was particularly evident when I had an unexpected and enforced stay in hospital at the time that Book 2 was being published.

A major feature of the series has been its eye-catching layout produced by the designers and artists who are, I trust, pleased with their imaginative results.

Finally, I must thank and pay tribute to Louise Martine who has masterminded the whole project and with whom I have had a very happy working relationship.

David Hillard
June 2009

Mental Strategies

The final chapters of *Junior Maths Books 1* and *2* have included material on Mental Strategies. To avoid repeating this information in *Book 3* it is now available as a free download from the website www.galorepark.co.uk with a short introduction included in this book.

Contents

Chapter 1: Introducing investigations

At the end of each chapter in this book you will find an investigation or puzzle for you to solve. Sometimes it will involve numbers only and sometimes there will be a pattern of shapes from which you will find a number pattern. Although each activity is different, there are some basic ideas that are worth looking at before you tackle them.

Investigating number patterns

Here are two columns of numbers.

What do you need to do, **each and every time**, to the number in **Column A** to make the number in **Column B**?

Column A		Column B
1	→	2
2	→	3
3	→	4
4	→	5
5	→	6

Did you add 1? If so, you are correct because

1 + **1**	=	2
2 + **1**	=	3
3 + **1**	=	4
4 + **1**	=	5
5 + **1**	=	6

Each and every time, you add 1 to the number in **Column A** to make the number in **Column B**.

Now look at these two columns.

What do you need to do this time to turn the number in **Column A** into the number in **Column B**?

Column A		Column B
1	→	2
2	→	4
3	→	6
4	→	8
5	→	10

If your answer is 'double' or 'multiply by 2', you are correct because

$$1 \times 2 = 2$$
$$2 \times 2 = 4$$
$$3 \times 2 = 6$$
$$4 \times 2 = 8$$
$$5 \times 2 = 10$$

The calculation you perform on the number in Column A, in order to make the new number in Column B, is often referred to as the **function**.

Some functions have more than one step.

What has happened here?

Column A		Column B
1	→	3
2	→	5
3	→	7
4	→	9
5	→	11

Let's look for a clue.

Look at the **difference** between the numbers in column B. It is 2 (5 − 3 = 2, 7 − 5 = 2, and so on). This suggests that it may have something to do with the 2 times table.

Make a new column (C) and write down the 2 times table.

What can you do to the numbers in Column C to make them match those in Column B?

Column A		Column B	Column C
1	→	3	2
2	→	5	4
3	→	7	6
4	→	9	8
5	→	11	10

The answer is 'add 1'.

So, in summary, we have **multiplied by 2** and **added 1** to the numbers in Column A to make the numbers in Column B.

$(1 × 2 = 2) + 1 = 3$

$(2 × 2 = 4) + 1 = 5$

$(3 × 2 = 6) + 1 = 7$

$(4 × 2 = 8) + 1 = 9$

$(5 × 2 = 10) + 1 = 11$

The function is 'multiply by 2 and add 1'.

Remember: To find the clue, look for the difference between the numbers in column B. If a times table has been used, the difference will be the same.

Examples:

What functions have been used here?

(i)   **Column A**   **Column B**

1	→	1
2	→	3
3	→	5
4	→	7
5	→	9

Hint: Remember to look at the difference between the numbers in Column B first.

The function is 'multiply by 2 and subtract 1'.

$(1 × 2 = 2) − 1 = 1$

$(2 × 2 = 4) − 1 = 3$, and so on

(ii)   **Column A**   **Column B**

1	→	5
2	→	8
3	→	11
4	→	14
5	→	17

The difference between the numbers in Column B is 3, so this suggests that it may have something to do with the 3 times table.

The function is 'multiply by 3 and add 2'.

$(1 × 3 = 3) + 2 = 5$

$(2 × 3 = 6) + 2 = 8$, and so on

Once you know what has happened you can find other pairs of numbers. For example, look again at Example (i) above. What would be the number in Column B if the number in Column A was 6?

Column A   **Column B**

6          $\longrightarrow$?

(Use the function you discovered earlier, that is, 'multiply by 2 and subtract 1'.)

? is 6 × **2** = 12 then subtract 1, so 12 − **1** = 11

? = 11

The number in Column B is 11

What would be the number in Column B if the number in Column A was 25?

Column A   **Column B**

25          $\longrightarrow$?

? is 25 × **2** = 50 then subtract 1, so 50 − **1** = 49

? = 49

Try the following example yourself.

Example:

Look again at Example (ii) on page 4. What would be the numbers in Column B if the numbers in Column A were 6 and 20? Remember to use the function you discovered earlier, that is, 'multiply by 3 and add 2'.

If the number in Column A is 6, the number in Column B is 20 because (6 × **3** = 18) + **2** = 20

If the number in Column A is 20, the number in Column B is 62 because (20 × **3** = 60) + **2** = 62

Inverse of a function

In the section above we worked out the function used to generate the numbers in Column B when we knew the numbers in Column A. We can also do this in reverse. That is, if we know the number in Column B, we can work out the corresponding number in Column A by using the **inverse of the function**. This means you **reverse** the calculation.

Function	Inverse function
×	÷
÷	×
+	−
−	+

Look at Example (i) on page 4 again.

The **function** in our first example was 'multiply by 2 and subtract 1'.

The **inverse** of this function is 'add 1 and divide by 2'.

Notice how you add the 1 first and then divide by 2

This is the complete reverse of the function. Imagine that you are reversing back through the commands issued by the function.

Column A		Column B	
5	→	9	Function is 'multiply by 2 and subtract 1'
6	→	11	Therefore inverse function is 'add 1 and divide by 2'
a	←	13	(13 + **1** = 14) ÷ **2** = 7 So a = 7
b	←	41	(41 + **1** = 42) ÷ **2** = 21 So b = 21

Try the following example yourself.

Example:

Look at Example (ii) on page 4 again. The function was 'multiply by 3 and add 2', so the inverse function is 'subtract 2 and divide by 3'. What are the numbers in Column A if the numbers in Column B are 23 and 65?

If the number in Column B is 23, the number in Column A is 7 because
$(23 - \textbf{2} = 21) \div \textbf{3} = 7$

If the number in Column B is 65, the number in Column A is 21 because
$(65 - \textbf{2} = 63) \div \textbf{3} = 21$

Exercise 1.1: Investigating number patterns

For each of the patterns (a) to (f) below:

1. Write down, in words, what you do to change the numbers in Column A into the numbers in Column B.

2. Find the value of the letters in each pattern.

(a) Column A		Column B	(b) Column A		Column B
1	→	3	1	→	3
2	→	4	2	→	6
3	→	5	3	→	9
4	→	6	4	→	12
5	→	7	5	→	15
8	→	a	7	→	c
b	←	17	d	←	36

(c)

Column A		Column B
1	→	5
2	→	7
3	→	9
4	→	11
5	→	13
9	→	e
f	←	53

(e)

Column A		Column B
1	→	5
2	→	9
3	→	13
4	→	17
5	→	21
10	→	i
j	←	101

(d)

Column A		Column B
1	→	2
2	→	5
3	→	8
4	→	11
5	→	14
15	→	g
h	←	59

(f)

Column A		Column B
1	→	0
2	→	2
3	→	4
4	→	6
5	→	8
16	→	k
l	←	98

Investigating shape patterns

This idea of number patterns can also be applied to questions with patterns made up of shapes.

These patterns of squares are made up of lines and dots.

By looking at the patterns, we can work out what the next patterns in the sequence will look like.

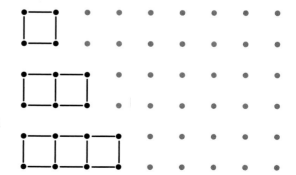

Example:

Draw the next two patterns in the sequence.

The next two patterns have 4 and 5 squares.

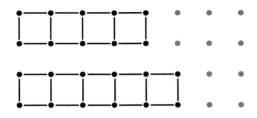

We can also record details of the patterns in a table like this one.

Number of squares	Number of lines	Number of dots
1	4	4
2	7	6
3	10	8
4	13	10
5	16	12

We now have a pattern of numbers like those we saw in the first part of this chapter. With this knowledge we can work out the functions that link:

● the number of squares to the number of lines; and
● the number of squares to the number of dots.

| squares | → | lines | multiply by 3 and add 1 |
| squares | → | dots | multiply by 2 and add 2 |

We can use these functions to answer questions.

Examples:

(i)   How many lines are there in the pattern with 8 squares?

Function is 'multiply by 3 and add 1' (squares → lines).

$(8 \times 3 = 24) + 1 = 25$

There are 25 lines in the pattern with 8 squares.

(ii) How many dots are there in the pattern with 25 squares?

Function is 'multiply by 2 and add 2' (squares → dots).

$(25 \times 2 = 50) + 2 = 52$

There are 52 dots in the pattern with 25 squares.

(iii) How many squares are there when the number of lines is 34?

This time we need to look at things in reverse by using the **inverse function** of squares → lines, which is 'subtract 1 and divide by 3'.

$(34 - 1 = 33) \div 3 = 11$

There are 11 squares when the number of lines is 34

(iv) There are 202 dots. How many squares are there?

This time we need to look at the **inverse function** of squares → dots, which is 'subtract 2 and divide by 2'.

$(202 - 2 = 200) \div 2 = 100$

There are 100 squares when there are 202 dots.

On the next two pages there are some questions for you to try.

Exercise 1.2: Investigating shape patterns

1. This pattern is made with vertical and horizontal lines.

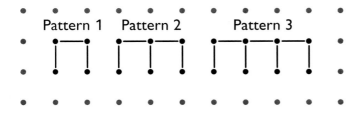

Pattern 1   Pattern 2   Pattern 3

(a) Draw patterns 4 and 5

(b) Copy and complete the table below.

Pattern number	Number of horizontal lines	Number of vertical lines	Total number of lines
1	1	2	3
2	2	3	5
3			
4			
5			

Tip: First work out the functions for:

pattern number   →   horizontal lines

pattern number   →   vertical lines

pattern number   →   total number of lines

and the inverse functions of each of these.

(c) How many horizontal lines are there in pattern 19?

(d) How many vertical lines are there in pattern 38?

(e) What is the total number of lines in pattern 41?

(f) Which pattern number has 71 vertical lines?

(g) Which pattern number has a total of 101 lines?

(h) What is the largest pattern number that can be made with 145 lines?

2. This pattern is made with lines and dots.

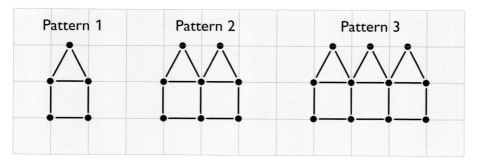

Pattern 1   Pattern 2   Pattern 3

(a) Draw patterns 4 and 5

(b) Copy and complete the table below.

Pattern number	Number of lines	Number of dots
1	6	5
2	11	8
3		
4		
5		

Tip: Work out all the functions and inverse functions first.

(c) How many lines are there in pattern 10?

(d) How many dots are there in pattern 12?

(e) Which pattern number has 101 lines?

(f) Which pattern number has 149 dots?

Note: You will find it helpful to have a calculator handy for some of the calculations you will meet in future activities.

Did you know?

There are 206 bones in the human body!

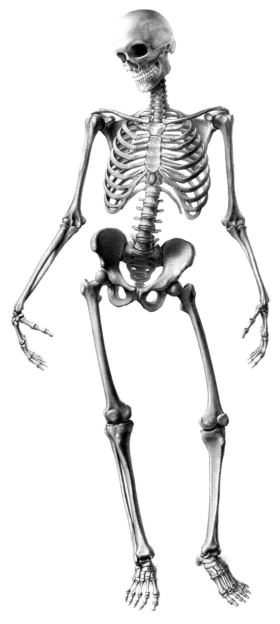

Chapter 2: The calculator

Calculators come in all shapes and sizes. They don't all require exactly the same approach to calculation. Whether you have your own calculator or whether everyone uses the same model, it is important to play with it to give yourself plenty of practice. We will cover some basic calculations in this chapter.

Remember: A calculator is never wrong. It's the person using it who makes the mistakes!

Getting started

Can you do the following on your calculator?

turn on/off

clear the display before starting another calculation

clear/delete an incorrect entry

add $\boxed{+}$

subtract $\boxed{-}$

multiply $\boxed{\times}$

divide $\boxed{\div}$

equals $\boxed{=}$

decimal point $\boxed{\cdot}$

Now let's try some simple calculations.

Examples:

Calculate:

(i)   27 + 4   27 $\boxed{+}$ 4 $\boxed{=}$ 31

(ii)   154 − 86   154 $\boxed{-}$ 86 $\boxed{=}$ 68

(iii) 24 × 17   24 $\boxed{\times}$ 17 $\boxed{=}$ 408

Examples (cont.):

(iv) 477 ÷ 3   477 ÷ 3 = 159

(v)   4.6 + 12.4 − 9.23   4.6 + 12.4 − 9.23 = 7.77

(vi) 8.3 × 1.5 ÷ 0.03   8.3 × 1.5 ÷ 0.03 = 415

(vii) 12.3 ÷ 4.1 + 34.7   12.3 ÷ 4.1 + 34.7 = 37.7

(viii) 5.6 × 6.4 − 52.6   5.6 × 6.4 − 52.6 = ⁻16.76
                             (**Note:** This gives you a negative number answer.)

If you are working out calculations with decimal numbers starting with 0, you can omit the 0 when inputting.

Example:

0.63 − 0.7 + 0.091   .63 − .7 + .091 = 0.021

Exercise 2.1: Integers and decimals

Calculate:

1. 46 + 183

2. 71 − 27

3. 26 × 8

4. 805 ÷ 23

5. 15 − 86

6. 56 − 134 + 97

7. 12 × 13 × 14

8. 540 ÷ 12 ÷ 3

9. 17 × 28 + 43

10. 246 ÷ 3 − 69

11. 3.86 + 12.4

12. 22.7 − 8.96

13. 6.3 × 1.7

14. 19.32 ÷ 0.24

15. 0.7 + 8.4 + 37.6

16. 138.7 − 15.9 − 86.4

17. 1.2 × 0.7 × 4.36

18. 64.8 ÷ 3.6 ÷ 0.18

19. 64.34 + 107 − 29.5

20. 147.3 − 28.61 + 2.73

21. 32.8 ÷ 0.4 × 13.6

22. 6.4 × 4.88 × 0.25

23. 4.3 × 8.7 − 19.6

24. 26.1 ÷ 0.9 + 0.73

25. 82.62 ÷ 1.7

Money

When you use a calculator for calculations involving money you must remember that sums of money are rather like decimals. Pounds come before the decimal point and pence after. Remember, there are always two figures for the pence part.

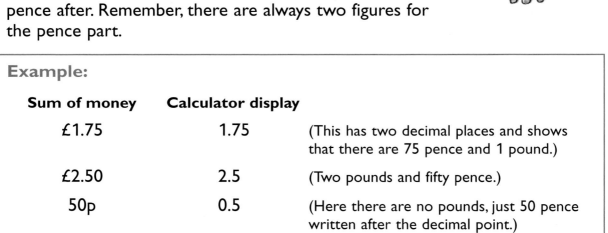

Example:

Sum of money	Calculator display	
£1.75	1.75	(This has two decimal places and shows that there are 75 pence and 1 pound.)
£2.50	2.5	(Two pounds and fifty pence.)
50p	0.5	(Here there are no pounds, just 50 pence written after the decimal point.)
£2.05	2.05	(This has two decimal places and means 2 pounds and 5 pence.)

When adding mixed sums of pounds and pence, be careful to enter any pence as 0.xx where xx is the number of pence.

Example:

£7.89 + 45p is input as 7.89 **+** 0.45 **=** 8.34

So the answer is £8.34

Exercise 2.2: Money

Calculate the following:

1. £1.63 + £2.85
2. £4.50 − £2.63
3. £2.75 × 6
4. £30 ÷ 4
5. £3.48 + 65p

6. £10 − 78p
7. £6.70 ÷ 5
8. £7.95 × 12
9. £5.83 − £3.78
10. 78p × 6

11. 63p + £1.87
12. £12 ÷ 8
13. £2.46 + £16.87
14. £7.50 − 78p
15. £1.85 × 8

16. 67p × 18
17. £21.75 ÷ 15
18. £100 ÷ 8
19. £42.50 ÷ 34
20. £4.40 + 76p + £15.84

Turning fractions into decimals

Since a fraction is really a division sum ($\frac{1}{4}$ means 1 ÷ 4), you can turn fractions into decimals very easily, using your calculator.

Example:

$\frac{1}{4}$ = 1 ÷ 4 = 0.25

Turning fractions into decimals can help you to compare the size of various fractions.

Example:

Put $\frac{3}{10}$, $\frac{7}{20}$ and $\frac{8}{25}$ in order of size, starting with the smallest.

First turn these fractions into decimals using your calculator.

$\frac{3}{10}$ = 3 $\boxed{\div}$ 10 $\boxed{=}$ 0.3

$\frac{7}{20}$ = 7 $\boxed{\div}$ 20 $\boxed{=}$ 0.35

$\frac{8}{25}$ = 8 $\boxed{\div}$ 25 $\boxed{=}$ 0.32

You should now be able to put the decimals in order easily.

0.3 < 0.32 < 0.35

So the order is $\frac{3}{10}$ $\frac{8}{25}$, $\frac{7}{20}$ (Use the original numbers in the answer.)

Sometimes you will find the display screen on the calculator completely taken up by the same figure.

For example $\frac{1}{3}$ = 1 $\boxed{\div}$ 3 $\boxed{=}$ 0.333 333 33 which is called 0.3 **recurring** because the 3 is repeated for ever.

It is written with a dot over the 3 ($0.\dot{3}$).

See if you can find some other fractions that behave like this.

Exercise 2.3: Turning fractions into decimals

1.   Write these fractions as decimals:

(a) $\frac{3}{5}$

(b) $\frac{7}{8}$

(c) $\frac{2}{3}$

(d) $\frac{19}{40}$

(e) $\frac{121}{200}$

2. Write these fractions in order of size, starting with the smallest:

(a) $\frac{3}{20}$ $\frac{9}{50}$ $\frac{4}{25}$

(b) $\frac{5}{16}$ $\frac{9}{32}$ $\frac{13}{40}$

(c) $\frac{1}{4}$ $\frac{49}{200}$ $\frac{123}{500}$

(d) $\frac{33}{80}$ $\frac{21}{50}$ $\frac{2}{5}$

(e) $\frac{3}{4}$ $\frac{29}{40}$ $\frac{7}{9}$

Brackets

When using a calculator, it is very important to press the buttons in the right order. If you don't then you may come up with some very strange answers. Your calculator may have some buttons that look like this.

$($ and $)$

These are called brackets. They help you to do the calculations in the right way. If there are brackets in the calculation you put them in as you come across them. Let's look at an example.

Example:

Use your calculator to work out $(7.4 + 4.1) \times 2.6$

The brackets in this calculation tell us that we must first calculate $7.4 + 4.1$ and then multiply the answer by 2.6

Pressing the bracket buttons in the order they appear will make sure it is calculated correctly.

$(7.4 + 4.1) \times 2.6 =$ $($ 7.4 $+$ 4.1 $)$ $\times$ 2.6 $=$ 29.9

Try this calculation without putting in the brackets:

7.4 $\boxed{+}$ 4.1 $\boxed{\times}$ 2.6 $\boxed{=}$ 18.06

You may get a completely different – and wrong – answer!

When you use a calculator to work out an answer, it is still a good idea to write down the stages in the calculation. Practise doing this, so that you get into the habit.

Examples:

Use your calculator to work out these.

(i) $9 - (12.2 \times 0.3)$

Input 9 $-$ $\boxed{(}$ 12.2 $\boxed{\times}$ 0.3 $\boxed{)}$ $\boxed{=}$ 5.34

Write down the stages, using your calculator to work out the calculations within the brackets:

$9 - (12.2 \times 0.3) = 9 - 3.66$

$= 5.34$

(ii) $(8.7 \times 1.6) - (13.65 \div 2.1)$

Input $\boxed{(}$ 8.7 $\boxed{\times}$ 1.6 $\boxed{)}$ $\boxed{-}$ $\boxed{(}$ 13.65 $\boxed{\div}$ 2.1 $\boxed{)}$ $\boxed{=}$ 7.42

Write down the stages:

$(8.7 \times 1.6) - (13.65 \div 2.1) = 13.92 - 6.5$

$= 7.42$

Exercise 2.4: Brackets

Calculate the following using the bracket buttons on your calculator.
Remember to write down the stages of the calculation as shown in the
examples above.

1. (4 + 6) × 3   30 ✓
2. 4 + (6 × 3)   22 ✓
3. 10 − (7 × 4) −18
4. (10 − 7) × 4 12 ✓
5. 18 + (9 ÷ 5) 19.8 ✓

6. (18 + 9) ÷ 5   5.4 ✓
7. 33 − (9 ÷ 6)   +31.5 ✓
8. (33 − 9) ÷ 6   4 ✓
9. (8.6 × 4) + 2.3   36.7 ✓
10. 8.6 × (4 + 2.3)   51.6

11. 4.7 − (3.3 ÷ 0.8)
12. (4.7 − 3.3) ÷ 0.8
13. (91.35 ÷ 10.5) − 9.6
14. 91.35 ÷ (10.5 − 9.6)
15. (6.2 × 3.7) + (2.88 ÷ 7.2)

16. (15.9 ÷ 0.6) − (2.7 × 1.8)
17. (5.4 + 2.9) × (4.2 − 1.7)
18. (38.7 − 7.2) ÷ (4.3 + 1.7)
19. 23.1 + (5.3 × 1.8) − 4.76
20. 6.4 × (4.2 − 2.7) ÷ 0.25

Approximation

It is sensible to make an approximation of an answer before you start a
calculation. This is true whether or not you are using a calculator.
An approximation is a carefully thought-through estimate of what the
answer should be.

You need to ask yourself whether your answer is sensible. If it is not, then
try the calculation again but also recheck your approximation. There are
many ways to approximate. Here are two examples:

Examples:

(i)   Calculate   (56 + 97) ÷ (133 − 85)

      Approximate   150   ÷   50

      Approximate answer   3

      Actual answer (using a calculator) is 3.1875

In the first example, you can see that the approximation made is quite close to the actual answer.

(ii) The manager of a clothes shop spends £1249.50 on buying his stock of new sweaters. The sweaters cost £24.99 each. How many sweaters did he buy?

First approximate the answer: £1249.50 is close to £1200
and £24.99 is close to £25

Using these approximations the number of sweaters is 1200 ÷ 25 = 48

The actual answer is 1249.50 ÷ 24.99 = 50

Exercise 2.5: Approximation

Give an approximate answer to each of the following:

1. 43 + 58
2. 989 + 427
3. 1000 − 703
4. 60 − 0.03
5. 1.8 + 7.3 − 2.9

6. 43 × 9
7. 58 × 2.1
8. 61.4 × 9.8
9. 806 × 0.52
10. 3.7 × 2.1 × 8.95

11. 29.7 × 29.7
12. 22.3 × 18.6
13. 80.7 ÷ 8.9
14. 337 ÷ 19.1
15. 119 ÷ 4.01

16. 29.3 ÷ 0.95
17. 101.3 ÷ 24.9
18. 15.21 ÷ 1.93
19. 33 ÷ 6.9
20. 987 ÷ 53.3

21. What is the approximate cost of 36 pads of paper at 99 pence each?

22. Tommy's car travels, on average, 5.89 kilometres per litre of petrol. Estimate the number of litres of petrol he will need for a journey of 120 kilometres.

23. Peggy filled the tractor with 29.6 litres of diesel which costs 90.3 pence per litre. Roughly how much did the diesel cost?

24. A can contains 330 millilitres of lemonade. Approximately how many cans are equivalent to 5 litres?
(**Remember:** There are 1000 millilitres in 1 litre)

25. There are 32 chocolates in a box. Each chocolate has an average mass of 28.75 grams. Estimate the total mass of the chocolates.

26. A coach is allowed to carry up to 61 passengers. Estimate the least number of coaches needed to take 1200 supporters to Wembley.

27. Estimate how many 39 pence stamps can be bought for £5.00

28. What is the approximate total cost of 2.5 kilograms of pepper which is priced at £19.93 per kilogram?

29. Gold has a mass of 19.3 grams per cubic centimetre. Estimate the mass of a 51 cubic centimetre gold nugget.

30. Jimmy Bowler works in London for 5 days a week. His daily ticket costs £8.15
Estimate how much he pays in fares if he works 48 weeks in a year.

Checking answers

Calculators are very useful for checking answers. You could redo a calculation to check, but you might make the same mistake again. A really good way to check an answer is by calculating the inverse.

Examples:

You calculate	Check the inverse
(i) 4792 + 8279 = **13 071**	either **13 071** – 8279 = 4792
	or **13 071** – 4792 = 8279

(ii) 7500 − 3873 = **3627**	**3627** + 3873 = 7500
(iii) 758 × 69 = **52 302**	either **52 302** ÷ 69 = 758 or **52 302** ÷ 758 = 69
(iv) 2088 ÷ 24 = **87**	**87** × 24 = 2088

Exercise 2.6: Checking answers

(a)   Use your calculator to work out the answer to each of the following.
(b)   Check your answer on paper using an inverse.

1.   38 216 + 9427

2.   41 216 − 8476

3.   726 × 39

4.   427 × 518

5.   6447 ÷ 21

6.   83 627 ÷ 241

7.   48.75 × 9.63

8.   489.966 ÷ 7.62

9.   32.6 × 11.3

10.   1806.25 ÷ 42.5

When you answer a word problem, remember to write down the calculation first, before you use your calculator.

Example:

What is the total cost of 250 books which are priced at £3.95 each?

250 × 3.95 = £987.50

Exercise 2.7: Problem solving

1. There are three villages in the Muddle Valley. The population of Upper Muddleton is 23 402, that of Middle Muddleton is 8926 and 12 219 people live in Lower Muddleton. What is the total population of all three villages combined?

2. A group of 32 teachers win £816 592 on Lotto. They share their winnings equally. How much does each teacher receive?

3. A tray contains 60 apples. 20 trays make up a stack. Orchard Fruits have 125 stacks in their warehouse. How many apples are there in the warehouse?

4. Assuming there are 365 days in a year, how many seconds are there in a year?

5. The length of the Equator is 40 075 kilometres. The distance from the Earth to the Moon is 384 403 kilometres. How many times going round the equator is equivalent to travelling from Earth to the Moon? (Give your answer correct to the nearest whole number.)

6. The results of the last election in Sparta East were as follows:

Pythagoras	43 217
Archimedes	27 938
Plato	9465
Euclid	2810
Majority	. . . . . .
Turn Out	. . . . . .

    (a) By how many votes did Pythagoras beat Archimedes? (This is called the **Majority**.)
    (b) How many voted altogether? (This is called the **Turn Out**.)
    (c) Altogether 90 127 people were entitled to vote. How many did not vote?

7. The results of the last election in Mathematica Central were as follows:

Newton	. . . . . .
Einstein	22 244
Descartes	8916
Euler	. . . . . .
Majority	7219
Turn Out	61 492

(a) How many votes did Newton receive?
(b) How many people voted for Euler?

8. Light travels at a speed of 299 792 kilometres per second. How long does it take the light from a star 40 million kilometres away to reach Earth? (Give your answer to the nearest second.)

9. Sound travels at a speed of 343.14 metres per second. How long is it before a rifle shot is heard if it is fired from a point 5 kilometres away? (Give your answer to the nearest second.)
    Note: There are 1000 metres in 1 kilometre.

10. Dobbins Garage takes delivery of 50 000 litres of petrol which cost £39 600
    Petrol is sold for 84.7 pence per litre. How much profit does the garage make on this delivery?

End of chapter activity: Odds and evens

1. Copy and complete the following:

   6 − 4 = . . .
   6 − 5 = . . .
   5 − 2 = . . .
   5 − 1 = . . .
   E − E = . . .   E is an EVEN number
   E − O = . . .   O is an ODD number
   O − E = . . .
   O − O = . . .

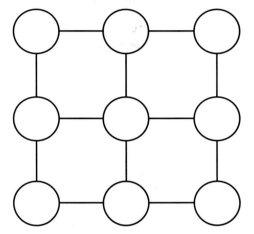

2. (a) Place the numbers 1 to 9 in the circles so that the difference between each pair of joined numbers is odd.

   (b) Do you notice anything about all the pairs of numbers that are joined?

   (c) Are there any other ways of arranging the numbers? If there are, draw them.

Did you know?

If a man's blood vessels were joined end to end they would stretch for a distance of 100 000 kilometres.

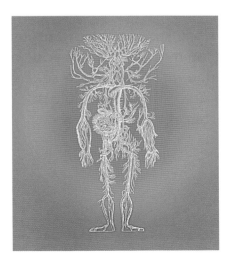

Chapter 3: Place value

A **million** is a very large number:

- A million football fans would need more than 100 Wembley Stadiums to seat them all.

- The straight line distance between Land's End (the most south-westerly point in Great Britain) and John o'Groats (traditionally considered the most northerly point of Scotland) is just less than a million metres.

- Birmingham has a population of about a million.

You already know that big numbers are written in blocks of three.

Hundreds	Tens	Units
9	4	7
nine hundred and forty		seven

The Thousands block has its own Hundreds, Tens and Units.

Hundred thousands	Ten thousands	Units (thousand)	(thousand)	Hundreds	Tens	Units
H	T	U		H	T	U
4	3	2		1	5	9
four hundred and thirty		two	thousand	one hundred and fifty		nine

Remember: There is a small space after the thousands block when there are five or more figures. In your maths exercise book you write one number in each square, so leave a blank square after the thousands block. The number above is written:

4	3	2		1	5	9

Writing large numbers in words

When writing a large number in words:

- Split the number into 3s from the right.
- Write the thousands block in words as it stands.
- Write the word **thousand** instead of the space.
- Write the **HTU** block.

Examples:

Write these numbers in words.

(i)   63 308

- This number has already been split into 3s.

Thousands block		HTU block		
6	3	3	0	8

- Thousands block: sixty-three.
- Write 'thousand' instead of the space.
- HTU: three hundred and eight

63 308 in words is sixty-three thousand, three hundred and eight.

(ii)   110 050 in words is one hundred and ten thousand and fifty.

Exercise 3.1: Writing large numbers in words

Write these numbers in words:

1.   4326

2.   127 503

3.   96 428

4.   11 011

5.   20 400

6.   320 106

7.   15 005

8.   700 000

9.   108 801

10. 9050

Writing large numbers in figures

When writing a large number in figures:

- Look for the word **thousand**.
- Write the numbers each side of it in **HTU**.
- Leave a small space in between the two blocks of numbers.

Remember: The last block of **HTU** must have three figures in it.

Examples:

Write these numbers in figures.

(i) Fifty-two thousand, four hundred and sixty-four

- Fifty-two **thousand**, four hundred and sixty-four
- Write fifty-two and four hundred and sixty-four in HTU:

Remember: The thousands block has its own Hundreds, Tens and Units.

Thousands block				HTU block		
H	T	U	and	H	T	U
	5	2		4	6	4

- Leave a space between the two blocks of numbers.

Fifty-two thousand, four hundred and sixty-four in figures is 52 464

(ii) Sixty-two thousand, two hundred and five in figures is 62 205

(iii) Four hundred and three thousand in figures is 403 000

Exercise 3.2: Writing large numbers in figures

Write these numbers in figures:

1. One thousand, four hundred and fifty-six

2. Seventy-three thousand, two hundred and nineteen

3. One hundred and forty-eight thousand, six hundred and seven

4. Twelve thousand and two

5. Seven thousand and ten

6. Two hundred and eighty-four thousand, six hundred

7. Nine hundred thousand and nine

8. Six hundred thousand

9. Fifty-one thousand, five hundred and eleven

10. Twenty-seven thousand

Place value and millions

When there are more than six digits we move into the **millions** block. This follows the same pattern as the thousands block:

● **Hundreds**, **Tens** and **Units** are used for the column headings.

Hundred millions	Ten millions	Units (millions)		Hundred thousands	Ten thousands	Units (thousands)		Hundreds	Tens	Units
H	T	U	(million)	H	T	U	(thousand)	H	T	U
1	2	3		4	5	6		7	8	9
one hundred	and twenty	three	million	four hundred	and fifty	six	thousand	seven hundred	and eighty	nine

● Millions and thousands are separated by a space.

1	2	3		4	5	6		7	8	9

Exercise 3.3: Place value and millions

Write down the real value of the underlined digit in each number:

1. 16 7̲28
2. 1̲43 269
3. 1̲ 432 657
4. 809̲ 528
5. 2̲4 350 075

6. 4̲30 000 000
7. 6̲1 000 000
8. 6̲10 000
9. 6̲10 000 000
10. 6̲ 000 000

Writing very large numbers in words

When writing a very large number in words where there are three HTU blocks, remember:

- the space on the left represents the word **million**; and
- the space on the right represents the word **thousand**.

Example:

40 312 060 in words is forty million, three hundred and twelve thousand and sixty.

Exercise 3.4: Writing very large numbers in words

Write these numbers in words:

1. 1 206 450
2. 2 450 070
3. 20 525 000
4. 13 013 103
5. 125 080 007

6. 4 600 000
7. 46 000
8. 460 000 000
9. 460 000
10. 46 000 000

Writing very large numbers in figures

When writing a very large number in figures, remember:

- the space on the left represents the word **million**;
- the space on the right represents the word **thousand**; and
- after the first space, each block must have three digits in it.

Examples:

(i)   Three million, four hundred and one thousand and sixteen in figures is 3 401 016

(ii) Twenty-seven million and nine thousand in figures is 27 009 000

Exercise 3.5: Writing very large numbers in figures

Write these numbers in figures:

1.   Two million, one hundred and fifty-three thousand, five hundred and six

2.   Sixty-seven million, one hundred and ten thousand, six hundred and fifty-four

3.   Nine hundred and thirty-eight million, two hundred and seventy-four thousand, six hundred and fifty-one

4.   Six million

5.   Three hundred thousand and twenty

6.   Thirty million, five hundred thousand

7.   Four million and four

8.   Sixty million, six thousand and sixty

9.   One hundred and eighty million, eighteen thousand and eight

10. One million, one thousand and ten

End of chapter activity: Arithmogons

1. Put the numbers 1 to 6 in the circles so that each side of the triangle totals 9

2. Now repeat the task, making the totals 10, 11 and 12

3. Did you find any pattern that helped you? If so, explain what you found.

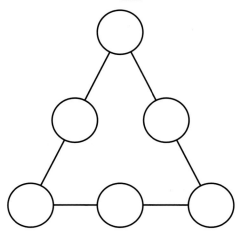

Did you know?

- In this country, it is reckoned **168** million cups of tea are drunk daily.
- **830** million Brussels sprouts are bought in the United Kingdom over the Christmas period.
- A total of **68 066 028** passengers used London Heathrow Airport in 2007

Chapter 4: Factors

A **factor** is a number that divides exactly into another number, leaving no remainder.

2 is a factor of 12 because 12 ÷ 2 = 6 with no remainder. All numbers have factors since 1 divides exactly into any number, but we will not worry about 1 for the moment.

We must look at the clues that tell us whether a number is a factor of another number. They are called the **rules of divisibility**.

The rules of divisibility

Here are some of the rules you can learn which will help your understanding of numbers. Make sure you learn your times tables, because they will help you understand these rules better.

Divisibility by 2, 4 and 8

● **All** even numbers have at least one even factor.

● Numbers that can be **divided by 2** are called **even** numbers and end in 0, 2, 4, 6 or 8

Examples: 30, 62, 74, 96, 138

● A number can be **divided by 4** if the last two digits of a number can be divided by 4 (remember, you can halve and halve again to divide by 4).

Example:

Is 4 a factor of 136?

　　The last two digits are 36, and 36 ÷ 4 = 9

　　So we can say that 136 is divisible by 4

　　This is the same as saying that 4 is a factor of 136

● A number can be **divided by 8** if the last 3 digits are divisible by 8 (remember, you can halve and halve and halve again)

Example:

Is 8 a factor of 2120?

The last 3 digits are 120, and $120 \div 8 = 15$ ($120 \div 2 = 60$

So we can say that 8 is a factor of 2120 $60 \div 2 = 30$

$30 \div 2 = 15$)

Exercise 4.1: Divisibility by 2, 4 and 8

Which of the following numbers are divisible

1.	by 2?	34	27	116	70
2.	by 4?	56	68	74	63
3.	by 8?	96	116	125	160
4.	by 2?	128	4587	2302	400
5.	by 4?	264	2484	3416	2008
6.	by 8?	680	375	2784	3160

Divisibility by 5 and 10

● Numbers that can be **divided by 5** end in 5 or 0

Examples: 45, 130

● Numbers that can be **divided by 10** always end in 0

Examples: 270, 20

Exercise 4.2: Divisibility by 5 and 10

Which of the following numbers are divisible

1.	by 5?	10	25	15	21
2.	by 10?	30	60	75	10
3.	by 5?	65	80	58	105
4.	by 10?	101	120	200	145

Divisibility by 3, 6 and 9

● A number can be **divided by 3 if** the sum of its digits is a multiple of 3

> **Example:**
>
> Is 3 a factor of 87?
>
> Add the two digits 8 and 7 together
>
> 8 + 7 = 15
>
> 15 is a multiple of 3 (3 × 5)
>
> So we can say that 3 is a factor of 87

● A number can be **divided by 6** if it is even **and** the sum of its digits is divisible by 3

> **Example:**
>
> Is 6 a factor of 48?
>
> 48 is even
>
> 4 + 8 = 12 and 12 is a multiple of 3
>
> So we can say that 6 is a factor of 48

● A number can be **divided by 9** if the sum of its digits is a multiple of 9

Example:

Is 9 a factor of 288?

2 + 8 + 8 = 18   and 18 is a multiple of 9

So we can say that 9 is a factor of 288

Exercise 4.3: Divisibility by 3, 6, and 9

Which of the following numbers are divisible

1.	by 3?	6	30	33	14
2.	by 6?	12	18	30	33
3.	by 9?	18	45	36	20
4.	by 3?	42	57	76	84
5.	by 6?	72	51	86	105
6.	by 9?	108	171	199	306

Divisibility by 20, 25, 50 and 100

- Numbers that can be **divided by 20** end in multiples of 20, that is 20, 40, 60, 80 or 00

Examples: 120, 340, 560, 680, 900

- Numbers that can be **divided by 25** end in multiples of 25, that is 25, 50, 75 or 00

Examples: 225, 350, 475, 600

- Numbers that can be **divided by 50** end in multiples of 50, that is 50 or 00

Examples: 450, 700

- Numbers that can be **divided by 100** end in multiples of 100, so the last two digits are 00

> **Example:** 1200

Exercise 4.4: Divisibility by 20, 25, 50 and 100

Which of the following numbers are divisible

1.	by 20?	40	85	60	100
2.	by 25?	50	75	120	125
3.	by 50?	100	150	345	200
4.	by 100?	100	250	400	601
5.	by 20?	80	110	200	330
6.	by 25?	200	160	175	325
7.	by 50?	400	180	505	250
8.	by 100?	400	650	800	2000

Exercise 4.5: Divisibility

1. What is the largest number less than 100 which is divisible by both 4 and 6?

2. What is the first three-digit number that is divisible by 4 and 10?

3. What is the largest number less than 1000 that is divisible by 20, 25 and 50?

4. What even number divisible by 9 is nearest to 200?

5. What is the first number that is divisible by 3, 4 and 5?

6. What number between 120 and 130 is divisible by 3 and has a digit-sum divisible by 4?

7. A three-digit number is divisible by 5 and the product (multiplication) of its digits is 35. What are the possible numbers?

8. What is the smallest number that is divisible by all the numbers 2, 3, 4, 5, 6, 8, 10, 20, 25, 50 and 100?

Pairs of factors

A **pair of factors** is two numbers which, when multiplied together, give you the required product.

> **Example:** 2 × 3 is a pair of factors of 6, 'the product'.

To find all the pairs of factors of a number you need to have a plan – don't just guess at random!

The plan is quite straightforward:

● Start with 1 × 'the number'.

● Then work through 2, 3, 4, and so on, remembering all the rules of divisibility you learnt above, until you reach a pair of factors you already have in your list.

Let's have a look at how this is done.

> **Example:**
>
> Find all the pairs of factors of 30
>
> 1 × 'the number'   1 × 30
>
> Try 2: yes, 2 is a factor because 30 is an even number   2 × 15
>
> Try 3: yes, 3 (3 × 1) is a multiple of 3   3 × 10
>
> Try 4: no, 30 can not be divided by 4
>
> Try 5: yes, 30 ends in 0   5 × 6
>
> Try 6: yes, 30 is even and the sum of its digits
>   is divisible by 3   6 × 5

However, we already have a pair of factors which includes 6, we don't need to write down 6 × 5 as well.

Remember: 5 × 6 is the same as 6 × 5

So the answer to the question 'Find all the pairs of factors of 30' is:

1 × 30,   2 × 15,   3 × 10,   5 × 6

Now try the following exercise, remembering to follow the plan described above.

Exercise 4.6: Pairs of factors

List all the pairs of factors of these numbers:

1.	12	6.	32
2.	16	7.	36
3.	18	8.	40
4.	20	9.	42
5.	24	10.	44
11.	45	16.	64
12.	48	17.	72
13.	50	18.	80
14.	56	19.	96
15.	60	20.	100

Square numbers and square roots

Some of the pairs of factors you found in Exercise 4.6 showed a number multiplied by itself. These are called **square numbers** because they can be drawn in the shape of a square.

Example:

16 is a square number because 16 = 4 × 4

It can also be written as 4^2 (4 squared)

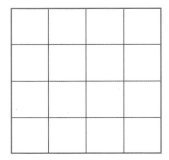

The opposite of a square number (otherwise known as the **inverse** of the square number) is called the square root. It is the number which, when multiplied by itself, gives you the square number.

Squares			Square roots		
1^2	=	1	$\sqrt{1}$	=	1
2^2	=	4	$\sqrt{4}$	=	2
3^2	=	9	$\sqrt{9}$	=	3
4^2	=	16	$\sqrt{16}$	=	4
5^2	=	25	$\sqrt{25}$	=	5
6^2	=	36	$\sqrt{36}$	=	6
7^2	=	49	$\sqrt{49}$	=	7
8^2	=	64	$\sqrt{64}$	=	8
9^2	=	81	$\sqrt{81}$	=	9
10^2	=	100	$\sqrt{100}$	=	10

Exercise 4.7: Square numbers and square roots

1. Draw a square pattern, like the one above, to illustrate each of the following square numbers.

   Write down the total number of small squares under each pattern.

   (a) 1^2 (d) 4^2

   (b) 2^2 (e) 5^2

   (c) 3^2

2. Write down these square roots.

   (a) $\sqrt{1}$ (d) $\sqrt{16}$

   (b) $\sqrt{4}$ (e) $\sqrt{25}$

   (c) $\sqrt{9}$

Prime numbers

Look at the following numbers. What happens when you try to find their factors?

   2   3   5   7   11

Each number has only **one pair of factors**, itself and 1

The factors of 2 are	2×1
The factors of 3 are	3×1
The factors of 5 are	5×1
The factors of 7 are	7×1
The factors of 11 are	11×1

These are called **prime numbers**.

Exercise 4.8: Prime numbers

1. Write down the prime numbers between 12 and 20 (there are three of them).

2. Use a copy of the square below to help you find all the prime numbers less than 100 (there are 25 of them).

   You might find it easier to cross out the numbers that are **not** prime (as in the first line of the square below).

   Use the rules of divisibility to help you.

   Note: 1 is **not** a prime number, it is a square number.

1	2	3	4	5	6	7	8	9	10
11	12	13	14	15	16	17	18	19	20
21	22	23	24	25	26	27	28	29	30
31	32	33	34	35	36	37	38	39	40
41	42	43	44	45	46	47	48	49	50
51	52	53	54	55	56	57	58	59	60
61	62	63	64	65	66	67	68	69	70
71	72	73	74	75	76	77	78	79	80
81	82	83	84	85	86	87	88	89	90
91	92	93	94	95	96	97	98	99	100

Prime factors

We have learnt that factors are numbers that are multiplied together.

Now let us look at **prime factors**. These are factors, but using only the prime numbers.

Example:

What are the prime factors of 12?

Factors of 12: 2 × 6   but 6 is not prime

3 × 4   but 4 is not prime

However, both 6 and 4 can be written as multiples of prime numbers:

6 = 3 × 2

4 = 2 × 2

So we can write 2 × 6 as 2 × 3 × 2

Or we can write 3 × 4 as 3 × 2 × 2

Usually we write the prime factors in order of size, smallest first.

So we can say that the prime factors of 12 are 2 × 2 × 3
(now **all** the numbers **are** prime).

The most common prime factors are 2, 3, 5 and 7, but don't forget 11, 13, and so on.

Just as it is best to follow a plan when you are looking for factor pairs, it is a good idea to use a logical method to find the prime factors of a number. One method is to use a **factor tree**.

Example:

What are the prime factors of 12?

- Start with the number in the middle of the page.

- Write down a pair of factors as the first 'branches'.

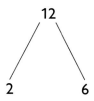

- Look at the numbers at the end of the 'branches'.

If a number is prime, leave it alone. (2 is prime)

If a number is not prime, write it as a pair of factors, using some more 'branches'.

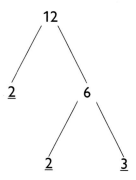

- Continue the process until all the numbers at the end of the 'branches' are prime. These are the prime factors of the number.

The prime factors of 12 are 2 × 2 × 3

Sometimes there is more than one way of finding the answer.

Example:

Write 24 as the product of prime factors.

Here are three different ways of arriving at the answer.

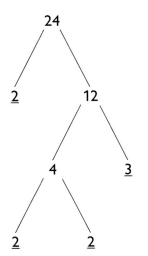
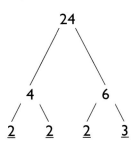
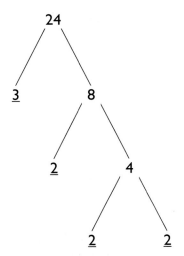

The prime factors of 24 are 2 × 2 × 2 × 3

Exercise 4.9: Prime factors

Find the prime factors of each of these numbers:

1. 16
2. 18
3. 20
4. 27
5. 28

6. 30
7. 32
8. 36
9. 40
10. 42

11. 44
12. 45
13. 48
14. 54
15. 56

16. 60
17. 63
18. 64
19. 69
20. 72

Ladder division is another method that you can use to find the prime factors of a number.

Example:

Find the prime factors of 300

- Start dividing by the smallest prime that you can.

2	3	0	0
2	1	5	0
3		7	5
5		2	5
			5

(Start with 2 because 300 is an even number.)

(Continue dividing by 2 until you cannot divide by 2 anymore.)

(Then divide by 3, 5, 7 etc as necessary.)

- Stop when you reach a prime number.

The prime factors of 300 are 2 × 2 × 3 × 5 × 5

When using ladder division, you can divide in any order, but you might find it useful to have a plan for how you will proceed.

Some people find this method easier with larger numbers. You should use whichever method you prefer.

Examples:

(i)

2	2	8	0
2	1	4	0
2		7	0
5		3	5
			7

2	5	8	8
2	2	9	4
3	1	4	7
7		4	9
			7

280 = 2 × 2 × 2 × 5 × 7

588 = 2 × 2 × 3 × 7 × 7

Exercise 4.10: More prime factors

Using whichever method you wish, find the prime factors of these numbers:

1. 80 *40, 20, 10, 8, 5, 2*
2. 84 *24, 4, 2, 3*
3. 90 *10, 9, 5, 2*
4. 96 *2, 12, 24, 8, 4*
5. 100 *5, 10, 2, 8, 6, 5, 4, 100*
6. 120 *60, 2, 5, 10, 4, 3*
7. 132 *2, 66, 33, 4, 3*
8. 140 *2, 10, 5*
9. 144 *12, 9, 2, 4, 72, 3*
10. 160 *80, 2, 5, 10*

11. 180
12. 196
13. 225
14. 360
15. 441

16. 576
17. 729
18. 850
19. 1000
20. 1225

Exercise 4.11: Summary exercise

1. From the numbers in brackets, choose all the factors of:
   (a) 138   (2, 3, 4, 6)
   (b) 234   (2, 3, 6, 9)
   (c) 375   (3, 5, 20, 25)
   (d) 430   (5, 8, 10, 20)

2. Write down all the pairs of factors of
   (a) 36   (b) 120

3. Write down the first five square numbers.

4. What is $\sqrt{64}$?

5. Write down the prime numbers between 20 and 40

6. Find the prime factors of

   (a) 60   (b) 96   (c) 189

7. Fiona has made some biscuits. She can pack them in bags of 6 or bags of 10 and have none left over. What is the least number of biscuits Fiona could have made?

8. Jimmy has more than 12 books. When he puts them in piles of three he has one book left over. If he puts them in piles of four he has two left over. What is the least number of books Jimmy can have?

9. Which of these numbers has 3, 5 and 8 as factors?

   115   150   240   265

10. Ramon's telephone number is made up of two of these numbers:

    150   170   260   375

    The first is the largest multiple of 20 and the second is the smallest multiple of 25

    What is Ramon's telephone number?

11. Answer the following questions using these numbers:

    4   8   9   10   12   17   21

    Write down:

    (a) a multiple of 6;

    (b) a number which has 7 as a factor;

    (c) a square number;

    (d) $\sqrt{16}$;

    (e) a prime number.

12. What factor do all of these numbers have in common?

    2   11   13   19

End of chapter activity: Magic dozens

Arrange the numbers 1 to 9 in the circles so that each side of the square adds up to 12

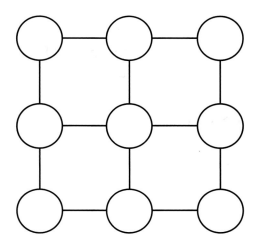

Draw as many different arrangements as possible.

Did you know?

Sound travels at a speed of 332 metres per second. It takes about $\frac{3}{10}$ of a second to hear a starting pistol that is fired 100 metres away.

Chapter 5: Number properties

In this chapter you will answer questions that will make you think about numbers in various different ways.

If you think about all the things you have learnt about numbers, you should find that you are able to answer these questions.

Note: In Exercise 5.1 * represents a digit.

Here is a reminder of the definitions of some of the terms used:

Sum means the result of adding two or more numbers.

Product means the result of multiplication (6 is the product of 2 × 3).

Difference means the result of subtraction (the difference between two numbers).

Exercise 5.1: Number properties

1. By giving several examples, show that these statements are true:
   (a) The sum of three odd numbers is odd.
   (b) Any odd number is double another number + 1
   (c) All multiples of 4 end in 0, 2, 4, 6 or 8

2. Find three consecutive numbers that add up to 39

3. What numbers less than 50 can be made by adding 3 consecutive numbers?

4. Find two numbers that give:
   (a) A sum of 11 and a product of 24
   (b) A sum of 15 and a product of 54
   (c) A sum of 7 and a product of 10
   (d) A sum of 5 and a product of 6
   (e) A sum of 19 and a product of 90
   (f) A sum of 40 and a product of 400

5. Find a two-digit number whose digits give:

(a) A difference of 7 and a product of 18

(b) A difference of 1 and a product of 20

(c) A difference of 5 and a product of 14

(d) A difference of 2 and a product of 8

(e) A difference of 7 and a product of 8

(f) A difference of 6 and a product of 0

6. Replace each * with one of the digits 1, 3, 4 and 8 so that the following statements are true:

(a) * * − * = 38

(b) 3 * − * 9 = 19

(c) 4 * + * 9 = 82

(d) 3 * + * 7 = 120

7. Find as many ways as possible to complete this multiplication:
** × * = 252

8. Arrange the numbers 1 to 9 inclusive in three groups, so that each group has a sum of 15

Use each number only once.

9. Replace each * with a digit so that the following statements are true:

(a) 1 * + * 7 = 32

(b) 3 * − * 4 = 4

10. How many groups of four odd numbers that add up to 20 can you find? The numbers within each group must all be different.

11. (a) What is the first odd multiple of 3 that is greater than 47?

(b) Write down a prime number between 29 and 35

(c) Write down a two-digit square number that is greater than 25 and the product of whose digits is 36

(d) Write down the number whose square and square root are the same.

12. Find as many as possible pairs of numbers whose product is 36

13. Find as many sets of three numbers as possible whose product is 24

14. Find a pair of consecutive numbers that add up to:
    - (a) 7
    - (b) 15
    - (c) 49
    - (d) 111
    - (e) 629

15. The following numbers are the result of adding three consecutive numbers:

    $15 = 4 + 5 + 6 \qquad 36 = 11 + 12 + 13 \qquad 90 = 29 + 30 + 31$

    $123 = 40 + 41 + 42$

    - (a) Do the four examples above have anything in common?
    - (b) Which of the following numbers can be made by adding three consecutive numbers?

      456   532   618   789   1234   3456

16. (a) I am a two-digit number between 30 and 60
    I am a multiple of 4 and the sum of my digits is 4
    Who am I?

    (b) I am a two-digit odd number between 30 and 60
    I am a multiple of 5 and the sum of my digits is 10
    Who am I?

    (c) I am a two-digit multiple of 3 less than 30
    The difference between my digits is 5
    Who am I?

    (d) I am more than 20 but less than 30
    There are 8 different numbers that are my factors.
    Who am I?

17. Find a two-digit odd number that is a square number and the product of whose digits is 8

18. Which two-digit square number is four times another square number?

19. By thinking about square numbers, explain whether 1234^2 will be an even or odd number.

20. Use the digits 1, 2, 3 and 4 and any operation to make the numbers 1 to 20

Example:		$6 = 1 + 2 + 3$
or		$6 = 2 + 4$
or		$6 = 2 \times 3$
or		$6 = (3 \times 4) \div 2$

End of chapter activity: Similar sums

Find ways of arranging the following numbers so that each row, column and diagonal has the same total.

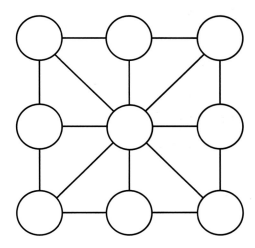

1 1 1

2 2 2

3 3 3

Now try the same with the numbers 4, 5 and 6

Try to think of another three numbers you could use.

Did you know?

Light travels at a speed of 300 000 kilometres per second. It takes just over 8 minutes for sunlight to reach the Earth.

Chapter 6: Decimals, fractions and percentages

We use decimals and fractions to mean 'how much' of something.

Will and Ali share a pizza.
They have $\frac{1}{2}$ a Margherita each.

Oliver weighs 3.4 kg.

A percentage is just a special kind of fraction. We usually use percentages to show 'how much' bigger or smaller something is.

This packet is 33% bigger than usual.

The prices of items in this shop are 25% less than usual.

In this chapter we are going to look at the relationships between decimals, fractions and percentages. Before we begin, it will be useful to remind yourself of the headings of place value and decimals.

Hundreds	Tens	Units	•	tenths	hundredths	thousandths
100	10	1	•	$\frac{1}{10}$	$\frac{1}{100}$	$\frac{1}{1000}$

Writing decimals as fractions: tenths

To write a decimal as a fraction, we put the number over a power of 10 (10, 100, 1000, …).

If we have **one** place of decimals to the right of the decimal point we have **tenths**.

Examples:

Write these decimals as fractions

(i) $0.3 = \frac{3}{10}$

(ii) $0.2 = \frac{2}{10}$

(iii) $0.5 = \frac{5}{10}$

Fractions in their lowest terms

We usually write fractions in their **lowest terms**. This means that we simplify the fractions by dividing the top and bottom numbers by the same factor, until we can't divide any more.

Let's look again at the answers to the examples above.

Examples:

(i) $\frac{3}{10}$ (This fraction is in its lowest terms so there is nothing more to do.)

(ii) $\frac{2}{10}$ (This fraction is not in its lowest terms. The top and bottom can both be divided by 2)

$\frac{2}{10} = \frac{1}{5}$

(iii) $\frac{5}{10}$ (The top and bottom can both be divided by 5)

$\frac{5}{10} = \frac{1}{2}$

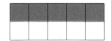

Writing decimals as fractions: hundredths

If there are **two** places of decimals, we have **hundredths**. Again, always express fractions in their lowest terms.

Tip: Always check to see whether you can divide by 2, 4, 5 or 25

Examples:

Write these decimals as fractions in their lowest terms.

(i) $0.09 = \frac{9}{100}$ (This fraction is already in its lowest terms.)

(ii) $0.61 = \frac{61}{100}$ (This fraction is already in its lowest terms.)

(iii) $0.06 = \frac{6}{100} = \frac{3}{50}$ (Divide by 2)

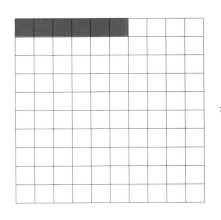
=
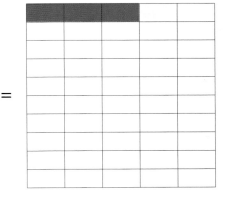

(iv) $0.26 = \frac{26}{100} = \frac{13}{50}$ (Divide by 2)

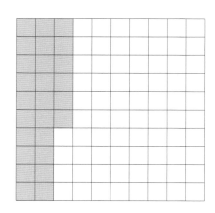 =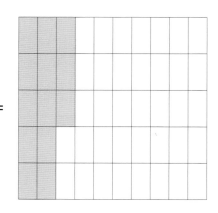

(v) $0.08 = \frac{8}{100} = \frac{2}{25}$ (Divide by 4)

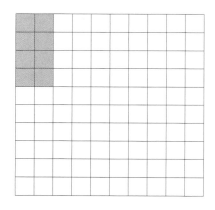 =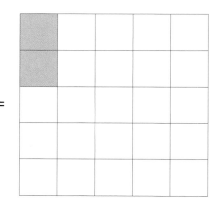

(vi) $0.28 = \frac{28}{100} = \frac{7}{25}$ (Divide by 4)

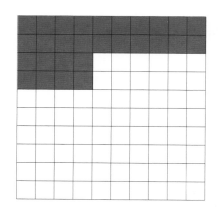 =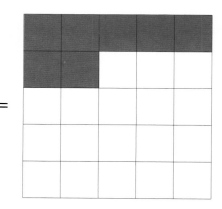

(vii) $0.05 = \frac{5}{100} = \frac{1}{20}$ (Divide by 5)

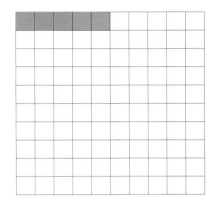 =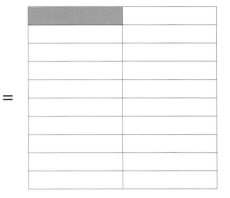

(viii) $0.35 = \frac{35}{100} = \frac{7}{20}$ (Divide by 5)

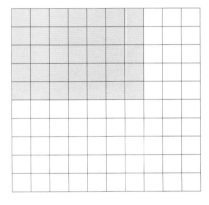 =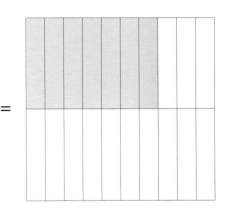

(ix) $0.25 = \frac{25}{100} = \frac{1}{4}$ (Divide by 25)

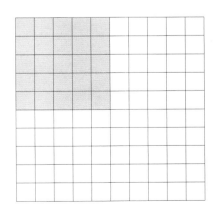 =

(x) $0.75 = \frac{75}{100} = \frac{3}{4}$ (Divide by 25)

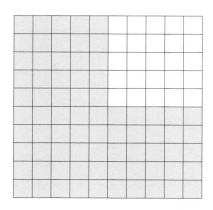

When we have a decimal which contains a **whole number**, the whole number remains untouched and we just deal with the numbers to the right of the decimal point.

Examples:

(i)   2.3 is written as $2\frac{3}{10}$

(ii)   3.85 is written as $3\frac{85}{100}$ and in its lowest terms $3\frac{17}{20}$

Exercise 6.1: Writing decimals as fractions

Write these decimals as fractions in their lowest terms:

1.   0.1

2.   0.9

3.   0.4

4.   0.05

5.   0.31

6.   0.16

7.   0.15

8.   0.46

9.   0.25

10. 0.01

11. 0.45

12. 0.02

13. 0.65

14. 0.04

15. 0.82

16. 0.88

17. 0.85

18. 0.72

19. 6.8

20. 7.18

Writing fractions as decimals

In Chapter 2 we saw how we could change fractions into decimals by dividing the top number by the bottom number.

Example:

$\frac{2}{5} = 2 \div 5 = 0.4$

	0 · 4
5	2 · ²0

For some fractions, however, we can use what we know about places of decimals to convert them to decimals.

Examples:

Write these fractions as decimals:

(i) $\frac{3}{10} = 0.3$ (We know that the heading for the **first** place of decimals is **tenths**, so we can write 3 tenths as 0.3)

(ii) $\frac{9}{100} = 0.09$ (We know that the heading for the **first two** places of decimals is **hundredths**, so we can write 9 hundredths as 0.09)

(iii) $\frac{61}{100} = 0.61$ (We know that the heading for the **first two** places of decimals is **hundredths**, so we can write 61 hundredths as 0.61)

Halves, fifths, quarters, twentieths, twenty-fifths and fiftieths don't share their names with decimal place column headings. However, 2 and 5 are factors of 10 and 4, 20, 25 and 50 are factors of 100. This means that fractions such as $\frac{1}{2}$ and $\frac{4}{5}$ can be written as equivalent fractions in tenths and $\frac{3}{4}$, $\frac{9}{20}$, $\frac{8}{25}$, and $\frac{7}{50}$, can be written as equivalent fractions in hundredths. It is then easy to write them as decimals.

Examples:

Write these fractions as decimals

(i) $\frac{1}{2} = \frac{5}{10} = 0.5$ (Multiply top and bottom of the fraction by 5)

(ii) $\frac{3}{4} = \frac{75}{100} = 0.75$ (Multiply top and bottom of the fraction by 25)

(iii) $\frac{4}{5} = \frac{8}{10} = 0.8$ (Multiply top and bottom of the fraction by 2)

(iv) $\frac{9}{20} = \frac{45}{100} = 0.45$ (Multiply top and bottom of the fraction by 5)

(v) $\frac{8}{25} = \frac{32}{100} = 0.32$ (Multiply top and bottom of the fraction by 4)

(vi) $\frac{7}{50} = \frac{14}{100} = 0.14$ (Multiply top and bottom of the fraction by 2)

As before, whole numbers remain as they are.

Examples:

(i) $2\frac{3}{10} = 2.3$

(ii) $5\frac{9}{20} = 5\frac{45}{100} = 5.45$ (Multiply top and bottom of the fraction by 5)

Exercise 6.2: Writing fractions as decimals

Write these fractions as decimals:

1. $\frac{9}{10}$

2. $\frac{2}{5}$

3. $\frac{17}{100}$

4. $\frac{9}{50}$

5. $\frac{3}{20}$

6. $\frac{4}{25}$

7. $\frac{1}{4}$

8. $\frac{3}{5}$

9. $\frac{7}{10}$

10. $\frac{19}{20}$

11. $\frac{1}{2}$

12. $\frac{41}{50}$

13. $\frac{21}{25}$

14. $\frac{1}{5}$

15. $\frac{17}{20}$

16. $\frac{2}{25}$

17. $1\frac{1}{10}$

18. $2\frac{1}{100}$

19. $5\frac{18}{25}$

20. $7\frac{3}{4}$

Writing percentages as fractions

Percentage, shown by the sign %, comes from the Latin 'per centum' which means 'out of a hundred'.

Whenever you see the % sign you can write the percentage as hundredths. So, for example, 10% is 10 hundredths ($\frac{10}{100}$). You may then need to rewrite the fraction in its lowest terms.

Examples:

(i)   Write 50% as a fraction in its lowest terms.

$50\% = \frac{50}{100} = \frac{1}{2}$ (Divide the top and bottom of the fraction by 50)

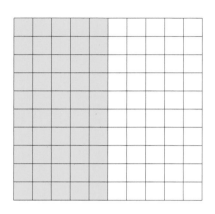

(ii)   Write 15% as a fraction in its lowest terms.

$15\% = \frac{15}{100} = \frac{3}{20}$ (Divide the top and bottom of the fraction by 5)

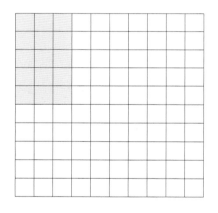

Exercise 6.3: Writing percentages as fractions

Write these percentages as fractions in their lowest terms:

1.   50%
2.   25%
3.   75%
4.   16%
5.   20%

6.   10%
7.   35%
8.   17%
9.   8%
10. 80%

11. 65%
12. 14%
13. 24%
14. 72%
15. 4%

16. 40%
17. 42%
18. 44%
19. 45%
20. 50%

Writing fractions as percentages

All fractions must be changed into their equivalent hundredths before we can work out the percentage value.

Example:

Write $\frac{9}{20}$ as a percentage

What do you need to multiply 20 by to give 100?

You need to multiply by 5

Remember to multiply both top and bottom of the fraction.

$\frac{9}{20} = \frac{45}{100}$

This can then be turned into the percentage 45%

Exercise 6.4: Writing fractions as percentages

Write these fractions as percentages:

1. $\frac{13}{100}$

2. $\frac{11}{50}$

3. $\frac{9}{25}$

4. $\frac{7}{20}$

5. $\frac{1}{10}$

6. $\frac{4}{5}$

7. $\frac{1}{4}$

8. $\frac{1}{2}$

9. $\frac{23}{50}$

10. $\frac{1}{5}$

11. $\frac{1}{20}$

12. $\frac{7}{10}$

13. $\frac{12}{25}$

14. $\frac{3}{4}$

15. $\frac{39}{50}$

16. $\frac{18}{25}$

17. $\frac{17}{20}$

18. $\frac{3}{5}$

19. $\frac{3}{50}$

20. $\frac{3}{25}$

Writing decimals as percentages

To write a decimal as a percentage, think of the decimal in hundredths, that is, with two decimal places.

Examples:

(i) Write 0.23 as a percentage.

$0.23 = \frac{23}{100} = 23\%$

(ii)   Write 0.7 as a percentage.

This time you have to remember to add a 0 after the 7 to show two decimal places.

$0.7 = 0.70 = \frac{70}{100} = 70\%$

Exercise 6.5: Writing decimals as percentages

Write these decimals as percentages:

1.   0.47

2.   0.36

3.   0.89

4.   0.6

5.   0.06

6.   0.81

7.   0.18

8.   0.5

9.   0.55

10. 0.05

Writing percentages as decimals

Since percentage is the same as hundredths, **two** decimal places are needed when writing a percentage as a decimal.

Examples:

(i)   Write 15% as a decimal.

$15\% = \frac{15}{100} = 0.15$

(ii)   Write 70% as a decimal.

$70\% = \frac{70}{100} = 0.70 = 0.7$

(iii) Write 7% as a decimal.

$7\% = \frac{7}{100} = 0.07$ (Be careful not to write 0.7)

Exercise 6.6: Writing percentages as decimals

Write these percentages as decimals:

1. 48%
2. 65%
3. 50%
4. 5%
5. 19%

6. 8%
7. 80%
8. 25%
9. 11%
10. 1%

Summary

To convert decimals to fractions

Remember: Always write your answer in its lowest terms.

1 decimal place
is **tenths**
$0.8 = \frac{8}{10} = \frac{4}{5}$ (Divide by 2)

2 decimal places are
hundredths
$0.45 = \frac{45}{100} = \frac{9}{20}$ (Divide by 5)

To convert fractions to decimals

Divide the top number
by the bottom number
$\frac{5}{8} = 5 \div 8 = 0.625$

Or turn the fraction into
tenths or **hundredths**
$\frac{3}{5} = \frac{6}{10} = 0.6$ (Multiply by 2)

$\frac{11}{25} = \frac{44}{100} = 0.44$ (Multiply by 4)

To convert percentages to fractions

Write the percentage as **hundredths** and then rewrite the fraction in its lowest terms.

$36\% = \frac{36}{100} = \frac{9}{25}$ (Divide by 4)

To convert fractions to percentages

Write the fraction in **hundredths**.

$$\frac{19}{50} = \frac{38}{100} = 38\%$$

(Multiply by 2)

To convert decimals to percentages

Use **two decimal places**.

$0.37 = 37\%$

$0.2 = 0.20 = 20\%$

To convert percentages to decimals

Write in **hundredths**.

$$39\% = \frac{39}{100} = 0.39$$

$$6\% = \frac{6}{100} = 0.06$$

Useful facts

Here are some very commonly used fractions, decimals and percentages which are worth learning:

$$\frac{1}{4} = 0.25 = 25\%$$

$$\frac{1}{2} = 0.5 = 50\%$$

$$\frac{3}{4} = 0.75 = 75\%$$

It is also helpful to know:

$$\frac{1}{10} = 0.1 = 10\%$$

$$\frac{1}{5} = 0.2 = 20\%$$

And if you really want to be on top of things:

$$\frac{1}{100} = 0.01 = 1\%$$

$$\frac{1}{50} = 0.02 = 2\%$$

$$\frac{1}{25} = 0.04 = 4\%$$

$$\frac{1}{20} = 0.05 = 5\%$$

Exercise 6.7: Summary exercise

This table shows equivalent fractions (in their lowest terms), decimals and percentages.

Copy it and fill in the gaps.

Fraction	Decimal	Percentage
$\frac{37}{100}$		
	0.71	
		43%
	0.25	
		75%
$\frac{1}{2}$		
		70%
$\frac{3}{10}$		
	0.9	
$\frac{1}{5}$		
	0.4	
		80%
	0.22	
		42%
$\frac{9}{50}$		
		16%
$\frac{11}{25}$		
	0.36	
$\frac{9}{20}$		
	0.35	
		65%

Exercise 6.8: Problem solving

1. Which is the larger of the following pairs?

   (a) 0.6 or $\frac{4}{5}$

   (b) 30% or $\frac{7}{20}$

   (c) 0.31 or 29%

   (d) 65% or $\frac{7}{10}$

   (e) 0.69 or $\frac{17}{25}$

2. Which is the smaller of the following pairs?

   (a) $\frac{1}{5}$ or 0.3

   (b) 90% or $\frac{47}{50}$

   (c) 0.51 or 50%

   (d) 23% or $\frac{3}{20}$

   (e) $\frac{3}{4}$ or 0.7

3. Write the following in order of size, starting with the smallest:

   (a) $\frac{1}{4}$ 0.23   24%

   (b) 0.6 $\frac{31}{50}$ 61%

   (c) $\frac{8}{25}$ 30%   0.31

4. Write the following in order of size, starting with the largest:

   (a) 0.3   4% $\frac{1}{20}$

   (b) 72%   0.68 $\frac{7}{10}$

   (c) 0.14   16% $\frac{3}{20}$

5. Feisal scores 57% in a test. Samira gets $\frac{3}{5}$ of the paper correct. Who got the higher mark?

6. Two shops sell a pair of ballet shoes at the same original price. Then both shops have a sale. Tutus offer 25% off the price and Pirouette give a $\frac{1}{5}$ discount. Which shop has the lower sale price?

7. Zak scores $\frac{13}{20}$ on an exercise. What percentage is this?

8. Richard is given 68% on an essay marked out of 25
   How many actual marks did he get?

9. Milly is given the choice of having her pocket money increased by either $\frac{1}{5}$ or 5%. Which choice gives her the larger increase?

10. In a 100 metre race Anne has completed 0.46 of the distance, Jane has covered 38% of the course and Catherine $\frac{11}{25}$ of it. Which girl is nearest to the finish?

End of chapter activity: Magic 15 [W]

Arrange the numbers 1 to 9 in three circles so that the total in each is 15

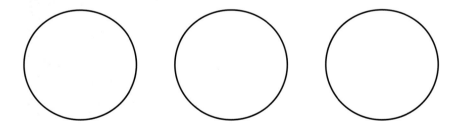

Find as many ways as possible of doing this.

Did you know?

When you sneeze, air comes out of your nose at a speed of around 100 miles per hour.

Chapter 7: Fractions of quantities

We know that a **fraction** means part of a **whole**. The bottom number tells you how many parts the whole has been divided into. $\frac{1}{2}$ for example is one whole that has been divided into 2 parts.

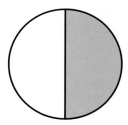

In this chapter we are going to look at how we can use fractions to talk about parts of a **quantity**.

Finding a fraction of a quantity: one part of a whole

In this example we have 6 apples in a basket and we want to work out how many apples is half of this number. We can write this as 'Find $\frac{1}{2}$ of 6'

To do this, we need to divide the 'whole' quantity (6 apples) into 2 parts.

We can write this as a division calculation: $6 \div 2 = 3$

So $\frac{1}{2}$ of 6 apples is 3 apples.

Here are some more examples.

Hint: We always divide by the number on the bottom of the fraction.

Examples:

(i) Calculate $\frac{1}{2}$ of 20

We need to divide 20 by 2

If you need to do your division in a frame then do so alongside.

$\frac{1}{2}$ of 20   = 20 ÷ 2

            = 10

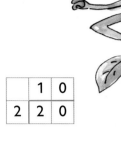

		1	0
	2	2	0

So $\frac{1}{2}$ of 20 is 10

(ii) Calculate $\frac{1}{4}$ of 68

In this example we need to divide 68 by 4

Once again, you can use a division frame if you need to.

$\frac{1}{4}$ of 68   = 68 ÷ 4

            = 17

		1	7
	4	6	8

So $\frac{1}{4}$ of 68 is 17

(iii) Archie has 12 bars of chocolate to give away. He wants to divide them equally between his 4 friends.

How may bars of chocolate will each friend get?

In this sort of word problem we need to think carefully about the numbers involved.

There are 12 bars of chocolate that need to be divided between 4 people.

We can write this as a division calculation:

12 ÷ 4 = 3

			3
	4	1	2

So each friend gets 3 bars of chocolate.

Exercise 7.1: Finding a fraction of a quantity: one part of a whole

Calculate:

1. $\frac{1}{2}$ of 24

2. $\frac{1}{3}$ of 42

3. $\frac{1}{4}$ of 36

4. $\frac{1}{5}$ of 75

5. $\frac{1}{6}$ of 90

6. $\frac{1}{7}$ of 91

7. $\frac{1}{8}$ of 104

8. $\frac{1}{9}$ of 108

9. $\frac{1}{5}$ of 270

10. $\frac{1}{6}$ of 420

11. Abigail gets half marks on a maths exercise which is marked out of 36 How many marks does she get?

12. There are 18 plums in a bowl. Mark eats $\frac{1}{3}$ of the plums. How many plums does he eat?

13. Balloons are sold in packets of 72 A quarter of the balloons are red. How many red balloons are there in a packet?

14. 'My Plaice' serves 85 people at lunchtime. One fifth of the customers order scampi and chips. How many order scampi and chips?

15. A sixth of the packets of crisps in a box of 96 are salty bacon. How many packets of this flavour are there?

16. A seventh of the 140 yachts in harbour have arrived from France. How many yachts have come from France?

17. Bessie bakes 120 small cakes. She ices an eighth of them. How many of them are iced?

18. Zac has 144 marbles of which a ninth are white. How many white marbles does Zac have?

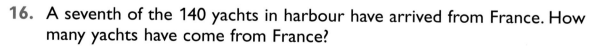

19. A group of children sit a total of 600 different exams. A quarter of the exams are awarded an A grade. How many exams resulted in an A grade?

20. A cross-Channel ferry has 927 passengers on board, of whom a third are children. How many children are there?

Finding a fraction of a quantity: more than one part of a whole

In the previous section we looked at simple fractions where there was just one part of a whole. For example:

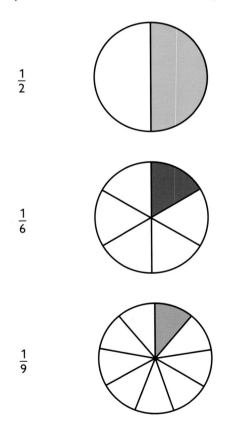

$\frac{1}{2}$

$\frac{1}{6}$

$\frac{1}{9}$

and so on.

Now we are going to look at fractions where there is more than one part. For example:

$\frac{2}{3}$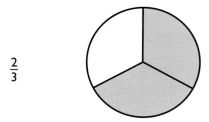

This means 2 parts, each $\frac{1}{3}$ of the whole.

$\frac{5}{6}$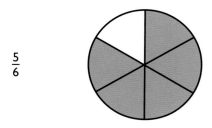

This means 5 parts, each $\frac{1}{6}$ of the whole.

$\frac{4}{5}$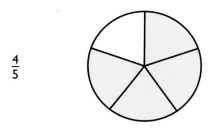

This means 4 parts, each $\frac{1}{5}$ of the whole.

In the following example we need to work out $\frac{4}{5}$ of a quantity.

First we work out what 1 part ($\frac{1}{5}$) is by dividing by 5 (the number on the bottom of the fraction).

Then we work out what 4 parts are by multiplying one part by 4 (the number on the top of the fraction).

Examples:

(i) Calculate $\frac{4}{5}$ of 40

Step 1: Work out what 1 part $(\frac{1}{5})$ of 40 is.

$\frac{1}{5}$ of 40 $= 40 \div 5$

             $= 8$

		8
5	4	0

We now know that $\frac{1}{5}$ of 40 is 8

Step 2: Work out what 4 lots of $\frac{1}{5}$ are:

$\frac{4}{5}$ of 40 $= 4 \times 8$

             $= 32$

$\frac{4}{5}$ of 40 $= 32$

(ii) Calculate $\frac{5}{6}$ of 60

Step 1: Work out what 1 part $(\frac{1}{6})$ of 60 is.

$\frac{1}{6}$ of 60 $= 60 \div 6$

             $= 10$

	1	0
6	6	0

We now know that $\frac{1}{6}$ of 60 is 10

Step 2: Work out what 5 lots of $\frac{1}{6}$ are:

$\frac{5}{6}$ of 60 $= 5 \times 10$

             $= 50$

$\frac{5}{6}$ of 60 $= 50$

When you have to solve a word problem involving fractions, remember to identify the numbers you need to use in your calculation carefully.

Example:

$\frac{2}{3}$ of a class of 15 are going to the cinema today.

How many cinema tickets does the teacher need to buy?

(There is a special offer on so the teacher goes free.)

We need to find $\frac{2}{3}$ of 15

Step 1: $\frac{1}{3}$ of 15   = 15 ÷ 3

                       = 5

		5
3	1	5

Step 2: $\frac{2}{3}$ of 15   = 2 × 5

                       = 10

The teacher needs to buy 10 tickets.

Exercise 7.2: Finding a fraction of a quantity: more than one part of a whole

Calculate:

1. $\frac{2}{3}$ of 18

2. $\frac{3}{4}$ of 20

3. $\frac{4}{5}$ of 15

4. $\frac{5}{6}$ of 42

5. $\frac{4}{7}$ of 84

6. $\frac{3}{8}$ of 72

7. $\frac{5}{9}$ of 81

8. $\frac{2}{5}$ of 70

9. $\frac{3}{4}$ of 92

10. $\frac{2}{3}$ of 111

11. $\frac{3}{5}$ of 145

16. $\frac{5}{6}$ of 300

12. $\frac{5}{6}$ of 192

17. $\frac{4}{5}$ of 360

13. $\frac{3}{8}$ of 144

18. $\frac{3}{7}$ of 294

14. $\frac{2}{7}$ of 238

19. $\frac{2}{5}$ of 195

15. $\frac{7}{9}$ of 126

20. $\frac{3}{8}$ of 400

21. A gym club has 80 members of whom $\frac{4}{5}$ are girls. How many girls are there?

22. 60 children have a choice of ice cream. $\frac{3}{4}$ of them choose a choc ice. How many choose a choc ice?

23. 130 trains stop at Bunton. How many trains are on time if $\frac{9}{10}$ of them are on time?

24. The rounders team won $\frac{5}{8}$ of its 16 matches. How many matches did it win?

25. $\frac{2}{5}$ of a packet of mixed nuts are cashews. How many cashews are there in a packet of 60 nuts?

26. $\frac{7}{8}$ of the staff at 'Bargains 4U' are aged under 30

How many of the staff of 112 are aged under 30?

27. $\frac{5}{6}$ of the 210 children at Grange School have a pet. How many children have a pet?

28. A sponsored swim raises £235

How much does the local children's home receive if it is given $\frac{3}{5}$ of the total?

29. Mr Pranav buys 144 tins of Fizzy. $\frac{2}{3}$ of the tins are lemon flavoured and the rest are orange flavoured. How many of the tins are orange flavoured Fizzy?

30. There are 40 girls in the Junior School. $\frac{3}{8}$ of them have brothers. How many girls do not have brothers?

Writing one quantity as a fraction of another quantity

Sometimes we want to write one quantity as a fraction of another. For example, we might want to know what 20p is as a fraction of 60p. In order to work this out there are two simple steps.

Step 1: Make sure the two numbers are in the same units (for example, if you are dealing with money, make sure they are both in pence) and write them as a fraction. The answer will give you the top number as a fraction of the bottom number.

Step 2: Cancel the fraction to its lowest terms.

Let's look at some examples where the numbers are already in the same units.

Examples:

(i)   Write 9 as a fraction of 30

   Step 1: There are no units because 9 and 30 are just numbers so we can just write the fraction:

   $$\frac{9}{30}$$

   Step 2: Write $\frac{9}{30}$ in its lowest terms.

   Look for a factor that goes into both 9 and 30 until you can't divide any further. In this case you can divide both top and bottom by 3 to give:

   $\frac{9}{30} = \frac{3}{10}$ (Top 9 ÷ 3 = 3)

   (Bottom 30 ÷ 3 = 10)

   9 as a fraction of 30 is $\frac{3}{10}$

(ii) Write 15 pence as a fraction of 25 pence.

   Step 1: Both numbers are in the same units, pence, so we can write the fraction:

   $$\frac{15}{25}$$

Step 2: Divide top and bottom by 5 to give the lowest terms.

$\frac{15}{25} = \frac{3}{5}$ (Top 15 ÷ 5 = 3)

(Bottom 25 ÷ 5 = 5)

15 pence as a fraction of 25 pence is $\frac{3}{5}$

Exercise 7.3: Writing one quantity as a fraction of another quantity (1)

Write the first quantity as a fraction of the second. Give your answer in its lowest terms.

	First quantity	**Second quantity**
1.	12	18
2.	28	40
3.	15 pence	30 pence
4.	25 pence	60 pence
5.	£4	£20
6.	£12	£30
7.	10 centimetres	35 centimetres
8.	48 centimetres	80 centimetres
9.	20 metres	30 metres
10.	25 metres	100 metres
11.	7 kilometres	21 kilometres
12.	24 kilometres	50 kilometres
13.	35 grams	50 grams
14.	130 grams	200 grams

	First quantity	**Second quantity**
15.	4 kilograms	28 kilograms
16.	30 kilograms	120 kilograms
17.	10 millilitres	17 millilitres
18.	400 millilitres	1000 millilitres
19.	15 minutes	40 minutes
20.	12 minutes	60 minutes

Let's now look at some examples where the numbers are not always in the same units. For example, you may have pence and pounds. Remember, if we want to write one quantity as a fraction of another quantity, the units for both quantities must be the same.

Examples:

(i) Write 15 pence as a fraction of £1

Step 1: The units are different. Change £1 to 100 pence (remember: 100p = £1). Then write 15 pence as a fraction of 100 pence:

$\frac{15}{100}$

Step 2: Divide top (15) and bottom (100) by 5 to give the lowest terms.

$\frac{15}{100} = \frac{3}{20}$ (Top 15 ÷ 5 = 3)

(Bottom 100 ÷ 5 = 20)

15 pence as a fraction of £1 is $\frac{3}{20}$

(ii) Write 24 centimetres as a fraction of 1 metre.

Step 1: The units are different. Change 1 metre to 100 centimetres (100 cm = 1 metre). Then write 24 cm as a fraction of 100 cm:

$\frac{24}{100}$

Step 2: Divide top (24) and bottom (100) by 4 to give the lowest terms.

$\frac{24}{100} = \frac{6}{25}$ (Top 24 ÷ 4 = 6)

(Bottom 100 ÷ 4 = 25)

24 cm as a fraction of 1 m is $\frac{6}{25}$

(iii) Write 400 grams as a fraction of 2 kilograms.

Step 1: The units are different. Change 2 kilograms to 2000 grams (1000 grams = 1 kilogram). Then write 400 g as a fraction of 2000 kg:

$\frac{400}{2000}$

Step 2: In this example, the cancelling is done in two stages.

$\frac{400}{2000} = \frac{4}{20}$ (First divide 400 and 2000 by 100)

$= \frac{1}{5}$ (Then divide 4 and 20 by 4)

400 g as a fraction of 2 kg is $\frac{1}{5}$

Reminder:

1000 millilitres = 1 litre

100 centimetres = 1 metre

1000 grams = 1 kilogram

90° = 1 right angle

100 cents = 1 $

Exercise 7.4: Writing one quantity as a fraction of another quantity (2)

Write the first quantity as a fraction of the second. Give your answer in its lowest terms.

	First quantity	**Second quantity**
1.	30 pence	£1
2.	5 pence	£1
3.	24 pence	£1
4.	20 pence	£1
5.	25 pence	£1
6.	6 millimetres	1 centimetre
7.	50 centimetres	1 metre
8.	80 centimetres	1 metre
9.	200 metres	1 kilometre
10.	500 metres	1 kilometre
11.	600 grams	1 kilogram
12.	250 grams	1 kilogram
13.	400 millilitres	1 litre
14.	50 millilitres	1 litre
15.	40 minutes	1 hour
16.	25 minutes	1 hour
17.	45 seconds	1 minute
18.	12 seconds	1 minute
19.	45°	1 right angle
20.	60°	1 right angle

	First quantity	Second quantity
21.	40 pence	£2
22.	75 cents	$3
23.	30 pence	£1.50
24.	5 millimetres	5 centimetres
25.	50 centimetres	2 metres
26.	400 metres	5 kilometres
27.	600 grams	3 kilograms
28.	120 millilitres	2 litres
29.	30 minutes	4 hours
30.	20 seconds	10 minutes

Summary

To find a fraction of a quantity

- Divide to find 1 part
- Multiply to find the total number of parts

Example:

What is $\frac{3}{4}$ of 48?

1 part ($\frac{1}{4}$) is 48 ÷ 4   = 12

3 parts ($\frac{3}{4}$) are 12 × 3 = 36

$\frac{3}{4}$ of 48   = 36

To write one quantity as a fraction of another

- Write the quantities as a fraction, making sure both numbers are in the same units
- Cancel to get the lowest terms.

Example:

Write 45 pence as a fraction of £3

Write 45 pence as a fraction of 300 pence: $\frac{45}{300}$

$\frac{45}{300} = \frac{3}{20}$ (Divide top and bottom by 3 first and then 5)

45 pence as a fraction of £3 is $\frac{3}{20}$

Exercise 7.5: Summary exercise

1. Calculate:

   (a) $\frac{2}{3}$ of 39   (f) $\frac{5}{8}$ of 120

   (b) $\frac{2}{7}$ of 28   (g) $\frac{7}{9}$ of 540

   (c) $\frac{4}{5}$ of 80   (h) $\frac{3}{4}$ of 600

   (d) $\frac{6}{7}$ of 91   (i) $\frac{5}{6}$ of 360

   (e) $\frac{3}{5}$ of 175   (j) $\frac{3}{8}$ of 1000

2. Write the first quantity as a fraction of the second.

First quantity	Second quantity
(a) 30	75
(b) 25 pence	£1
(c) 80 pence	£4

	First quantity	**Second quantity**
(d)	60 centimetres	1 metre
(e)	8 millimetres	5 centimetres
(f)	800 metres	2 kilometres
(g)	450 grams	1 kilogram
(h)	50 minutes	1 hour
(i)	80 pence	£2.40
(j)	30 cents	$1.50

End of chapter activity: Number neighbours

In these arithmogons, the number in each square equals the sum of the two numbers in circles on either side of it.

Example:

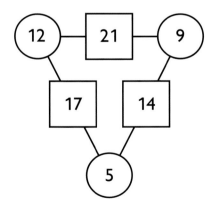

Copy and complete these arithmogons.

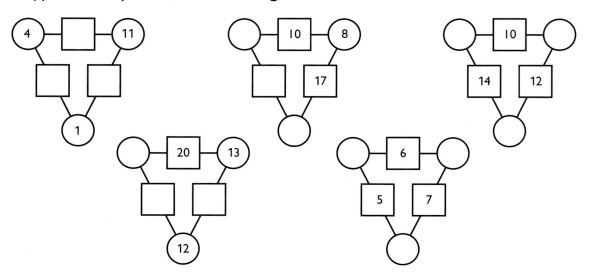

Did you know?

If each count was a second long, it would take about 12 days to count to a million and about 32 years to count to a billion.

Chapter 8: Percentage

As we saw in Chapter 6, **percentage (%)** means '**out of 100**'. A percentage is a part of the whole where 100% represents the whole.

Examples:

(i)   If 60% of a class are boys then 40% are girls. (60 + 40 = 100)

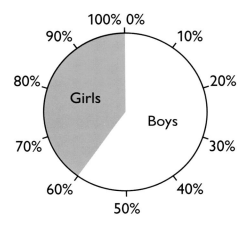

(ii)   Edward achieved 80% in his maths exam result.
(80 marks out of a possible 100 marks)

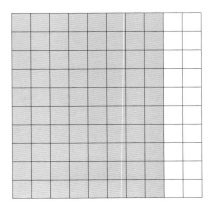

(iii) If 85% of the children have a pencil then 15% do not have a pencil.
(100 − 85 = 15)

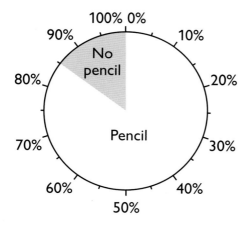

Percentages can be very simply thought of as fractions.

$1\% = \frac{1}{100}$ 1 out of 100

From the examples above:

(i) $60\% = \frac{60}{100}$ and $40\% = \frac{40}{100}$

(ii) $80\% = \frac{80}{100}$

(iii) $85\% = \frac{85}{100}$ and $15\% = \frac{15}{100}$

Finding one quantity as a percentage of another

In Chapter 7 you learnt how to write one quantity as a **fraction** of another quantity.

To write a quantity as a **percentage** of another quantity we first write the fraction and then multiply or divide both the numbers so that the bottom number is 100 (because 'percentage' means 'out of 100').

Remember: To keep the fraction equivalent (the same), whatever you do to the bottom number you must also do to the top.

We can then write the top number as a percentage (the 100 becomes %).

Examples:

(i) Write 3 as a percentage of 10

First write 3 as a fraction of 10:

$\frac{3}{10}$

Then multiply top and bottom by 10 so that the bottom number is 100:

$\frac{3}{10} = \frac{30}{100}$

Now we can write the top number as a percentage

$\frac{30}{100} = 30\%$

3 as a percentage of 10 is 30%

(ii) Write 11 as a percentage of 20

$\frac{11}{20} = \frac{55}{100}$ (Multiply by 5)

    $= 55\%$

(iii) Write 6 as a percentage of 25

$\frac{6}{25} = \frac{24}{100}$ (Multiply by 4)

    $= 24\%$

(iv) What is 30p as a percentage of £2?

$\frac{30p}{£2} = \frac{30}{200}$ (Write both numbers in pence.)

$\frac{30}{200} = \frac{15}{100}$ (Divide by 2)

    $= 15\%$

(v) What is 1.5 m as a percentage of 5 m?

$\frac{1.5\ m}{5\ m} = \frac{150}{500}$ (Write both numbers in centimetres to get rid of the decimals.)

$\frac{150}{500} = \frac{30}{100}$ (Divide by 5)

    $= 30\%$

Exercise 8.1: One quantity as a percentage of another

1. Write the first quantity as a percentage of the second:

	First quantity	Second quantity
(a)	7	10
(b)	17	50
(c)	23	25
(d)	4	5
(e)	12	20
(f)	40p	£8
(g)	£1.80	£3
(h)	27 mm	5 cm
(i)	80 cm	2 m
(j)	480 g	2 kg

2. 4 pencils in a box of 10 are red. What percentage of the pencils is red?

3. 9 children in a class of 20 are girls. What percentage of the class is girls?

4. 5 out of a group of 25 monkeys are chimpanzees. What percentage of the monkeys are chimpanzees?

5. 1 in every 4 cars has satellite navigation. What percentage of cars has this system?

6. Which is the higher mark, 39 out of 50 or 76%?

7. Charlie spends £600 on a holiday. His accommodation costs £270. What percentage of the total cost does this represent?

8. Gussie buys a hair band for 80 pence. She pays with a £2 coin. What percentage of the money does she spend?

9. Tom earns £25 a week as a paper boy. In January he was given an increase of £2.50. What was his percentage increase?

10. There are 200 children at Uptown Lower School. 164 of them live within 5 kilometres of the school. What percentage lives within 5 kilometres?

11. A roll of tape is 5 metres long.

    (a) George uses 50 centimetres to wrap a packet. What percentage of the roll is this?

    (b) Simone needs 150 centimetres to wrap her parcel. What percentage of a roll is this?

    (c) Terry needs 3.8 metres to wrap her box. What percentage of the roll is this?

12. A can of Fizzy contains 330 millilitres. What percentage of a litre (1000 ml) is this?

13. Jenny's £3 train fare is increased by 45 pence. What is the percentage increase?

14. A suit is originally priced at £500
    In a sale the price is reduced by £175
    What was the percentage decrease?

15. Mr Checker pays £1200 tax when he earns £6000
    What is the percentage rate at which tax is paid?

50%, 25% and 75%

You will come across certain percentages quite frequently so you should make sure you understand exactly what they mean.

Let's start by looking more closely at 50%.

50% = $\frac{50}{100}$ (We can write this in its lowest terms by dividing the top and bottom numbers by 50)

    = $\frac{1}{2}$ (A very familiar fraction!)

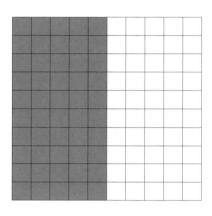

Now let us look at 25% and 75%

25% = $\frac{25}{100}$ (Write in its lowest terms by dividing the top and bottom numbers by 25)

    = $\frac{1}{4}$ (One quarter)

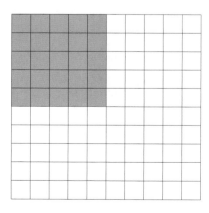

$75\% = \frac{75}{100}$ (Divide top and bottom by 25)

$= \frac{3}{4}$ (Three quarters)

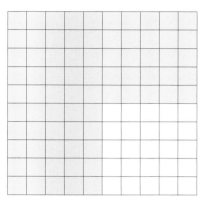

We can use what we have learnt about these percentages to find 50%, 25% and 75% of a quantity.

Examples:

(i)   What is 50% of 28?

50% is the same as a half. To find one half of a quantity we divide by 2

50% of 28 $= \frac{1}{2} \times 28$

$= 28 \div 2$

$= 14$

You should be able to do this in your head. If you can't, write it out like this:

		1	4
2	2	8	

50% of 28 $= 14$

(ii)   What is 25% of £32?

25% is the same as one quarter. To find one quarter of a quantity we divide by 4, or by 2 and then by 2 again.

25% of 32 $= \frac{1}{4}$ of 32

$= 32 \div 4$ (32 ÷ 2 = 16 then 16 ÷ 2 = 8)

$= 8$

25% of £32 = £8   (Remember to put the correct units in your answer, in this case £s.)

(iii) What is 75% of 160 kg?

75% is the same as three quarters. To find three quarters of a quantity, we first find one quarter, and then multiply that by three.

Step 1: $\frac{1}{4}$ of 160 $= 160 \div 4$

$= 40$

Step 2: 3 lots of $\frac{1}{4} = 3 \times 40$

$= 120$

75% of 160 kg $= 120$ kg

Exercise 8.2: 50%, 25% and 75%

1. Calculate 50% of:
    (a) 30
    (b) 124
    (c) £60
    (d) $250
    (e) 850 ml

    (f) £8.40
    (g) £1.36
    (h) £5.00
    (i) $7.50
    (j) 9 cm

2. Calculate 25% of:
    (a) 120
    (b) 48
    (c) £80
    (d) £36
    (e) 140 m

    (f) £4.60
    (g) £16.40
    (h) £6.00
    (i) £2.00
    (j) 2 m

3. Calculate 75% of:
    (a) 24
    (b) 60
    (c) 200
    (d) £40
    (e) £600

    (f) £2.40
    (g) £4.60
    (h) £9.00
    (i) 8 m
    (j) 5 kg

Percentage: 10%

$10\% = \frac{10}{100} = \frac{1}{10}$

The easiest way to find 10% of a quantity is to divide by 10

Think carefully about **place value** (page 28).

Remember, when **dividing** by **10** the figures move **1 place** to the **right**.

Examples:

(i)   10% of 70   = 70 ÷ 10
                    = 7

(ii)   10% of £90   = 90 ÷ 10
                    = £9

(iii) 10% of 120   = 120 ÷ 10
                    = 12

(iv) 10% of £360 = 360 ÷ 10
                    = £36

(v)   10% of 400   = 400 ÷ 10
                    = 40

(vi) 10% of £700 = 700 ÷ 10
                    = £70

(vii) 10% of 27   = 27 ÷ 10
                    = 2.7

(viii) 10% of £35   = 35 ÷ 10
                    = £3.50

(ix) 10% of 8   = 8 ÷ 10
                    = 0.8

(x)   10% of £4   = 4 ÷ 10
                    = £0.40 or 40p

(xi) 10% of £2.50 = 2.50 ÷ 10
                    = £0.25 or 25p

Exercise 8.3: 10%

Calculate 10% of:

1. 60
2. 250
3. 46
4. 5
5. £600

6. 200 m
7. 900 g
8. £70
9. 40 kg
10. 80 *l*

11. £75
12. £2.80
13. £6.30
14. £12.50
15. $27.50

16. 45 kg
17. 15 cm
18. 90p
19. 50p
20. £3.50

Multiples of 10%

To find multiples of 10% such as 20%, 30%, 40%, and so on, **find 10%** and **multiply**.

Examples:

(i) Calculate 60% of 80
   10% of 80 = 8
   60% of 80 = 8 × 6   (Multiply by 6 because 10 × 6 = 60)
              = 48

(ii) Calculate 30% of £45
   10% of £45 = £4.50
   30% of £45 = £4.50 × 3   (Multiply by 3 because 10 × 3 = 30)
              = £13.50

(iii) Calculate 70% of £2.50

10% of £2.50 = 25p

70% of £2.50 = 25p × 7

= £1.75

Exercise 8.4: Multiples of 10%

Calculate:

1. 20% of (a) 60 (b) £90 (c) £3.50 (d) £4

2. 30% of (a) 30 (b) £40 (c) £4.50 (d) £6

3. 40% of (a) 40 (b) £200 (c) £1.20 (d) £8

4. 60% of (a) 80 (b) £150 (c) £8.50 (d) £9

5. 70% of (a) 50 (b) £80 (c) £2.40 (d) £10

6. 80% of (a) 70 (b) £120 (c) £1.80 (d) £3

7. 90% of (a) 150 (b) £300 (c) £1.20 (d) £5

Fractions of 10%

To find 5%, **find 10%** and **divide by 2** $(10 \div 2 = 5$ so $5\% = \frac{1}{2}$ of 10%)

To find $2\frac{1}{2}$% **find 10%** and **divide by 2
and then by 2 again** $(5 \div 2 = 2\frac{1}{2}$ so $2\frac{1}{2}\% = \frac{1}{2}$ of 5%)

Examples:

(i) What is 5% of £80?

10% of £80 = £8

5% of 80% = $\frac{1}{2}$ of £8

= £4

(ii)   What is $2\frac{1}{2}\%$ of £120?

10% of £120 = £12

5% of £120 = $\frac{1}{2}$ of £12   (Halve 10% to give 5%)

= £6

$2\frac{1}{2}\%$ of £120 = $\frac{1}{2}$ of £6   (Halve 5% to give $2\frac{1}{2}\%$)

= £3

$2\frac{1}{2}\%$ of £120 = £3

Exercise 8.5: Fractions of 10%

1.   Calculate 5% of:

(a) 40

(b) 180

(c) 260

(d) £60

(e) £30

(f) £42

(g) £128

(h) £8.00

(i) £5.00

(j) £2.40

(k) £3.80

(l) £21.60

(m) 400 kg

(n) 920 m

(o) 1200 *l*

2.   Calculate $2\frac{1}{2}\%$ of:

(a) 80

(b) 320

(c) 280

(d) £120

(e) £50

(f) £30

(g) £1.60

(h) £4.80

(i) £12.40

(j) £20

Further percentages

You can use 10% as your starting point for finding very many percentages.
Here are some examples:

Examples:

(i)   35% of £40   (Think of 35% as 10% + 10% +10% + 5%)

       10% of £40   = 40 ÷ 10   (First find 10%)

                      = £4

       30% of £40   = £4 × 3   (To find 30%, multiply 10% by 3)

                      = £12

       5% of £40   = 4 ÷ 2   (To find 5%, divide 10% by 2)

                      = £2

       35% of £40   = £12 + £2   (Finally, to find 35%, add 30% and 5%)

                      = £14

(ii) $42\frac{1}{2}$% of £7.20   (Think of $42\frac{1}{2}$% as 10% + 10% +10% + 10% + $2\frac{1}{2}$%)

       10% of £7.20   = £7.20 ÷ 10   (First find 10%)

                      = £0.72 or 72p   (Remember, to divide by 10, move the digits one place to the right.)

       40% of £7.20   = 72p × 4   (To find 40%, multiply 10% by 4)

                      = 288p or £2.88

       5% of £7.20   = 72p ÷ 2   (To find $2\frac{1}{2}$% first find 5% by dividing 10% by 2…)

                      = 36p

       $2\frac{1}{2}$% of £7.20   = 36p ÷ 2   (…and then divide 5% by 2)

                      = 18p

       $42\frac{1}{2}$% of £7.20 = £2.88 + 18p   (Finally, to find $42\frac{1}{2}$%, add 40% and $2\frac{1}{2}$%)

                      = £3.06

Exercise 8.6: Further percentages

Calculate:

1. 15% of 60
2. 35% of 40
3. 45% of 120
4. 55% of 140
5. 65% of 80

6. 85% of 20
7. 95% of 160
8. $32\frac{1}{2}$% of 40
9. 35% of £12
10. 85% of £24

11. 15% of £48
12. 55% of £27
13. 65% of £6.40
14. $22\frac{1}{2}$% of £12
15. $12\frac{1}{2}$% of £4

Value Added Tax (VAT)

You might have heard about something called Value Added Tax (VAT). This is an extra amount of money that is charged on top of the value of most things we buy. The government collects this money and uses it to run the country.

Shopkeepers work out the amount of VAT they are going to charge by using a percentage value. The most common rate of VAT is $17\frac{1}{2}$%

We can think of $17\frac{1}{2}$% as 10% + 5% + $2\frac{1}{2}$%

Examples:

(i) What is the VAT charged on goods valued at £80?

This means the same as 'what is $17\frac{1}{2}$% of £80?'

10% of £80 = £8

+ 5% of £80 = £4   ($\frac{1}{2}$ of £8 because 5% is half of 10%)

+ $2\frac{1}{2}$% of £80 = £2   ($\frac{1}{2}$ of £4 because $2\frac{1}{2}$% is half of 5%)

$17\frac{1}{2}$% (VAT) = £14   (£8 + £4 + £2)

(ii) What is the VAT charged on goods valued at £56?

This means the same as 'what is $17\frac{1}{2}$% of £56?'

10% of £56 = £5.60

+ 5% of £56 = £2.80   ($\frac{1}{2}$ of £5.60)

+ $2\frac{1}{2}$% of £56 = £1.40   ($\frac{1}{2}$ of £2.80)

$17\frac{1}{2}$% (VAT) = £9.80   (£5.60 + £2.80 + £1.40)

Exercise 8.7: Value Added Tax (VAT)

Calculate $17\frac{1}{2}$% of:

1. £40
2. £280
3. £160
4. £140
5. £30

6. £36
7. £108
8. £64
9. £1.20
10. £3.60

11. £16.80
12. £48.80
13. £72.40
14. £91.60
15. £124.80

Exercise 8.8: Problem solving (1)

1. 40% of a class are girls. What percentage of the class are boys?

2. 82% of children eat fresh vegetables for lunch. What percentage of children do not eat fresh vegetables?

3. Richard gets 50% on a test marked out of 40 marks. How many marks does he score?

4. Jane eats 25% of a 200 gram bar of chocolate. How many grams of chocolate are left over?

5. 75% of the 160 boys at school have a sister. How many boys have a sister?

6. There are 60 apples in a box of which 10% are uneatable because they are too bruised. How many of the apples can be eaten?

7. Carlo's bill at the Pizza Parlour is £27.50
    He leaves a tip which is 10% of the bill. How much tip does he leave?

8. There are 60 chocolates in a box of which 45% have toffee centres. How many chocolates have toffee centres?

9. 25% of a packet of balloons are coloured red. If there are 50 red balloons what is the total number of balloons in the packet?

10. A group of 120 visits the Tower of London. 10% are adults and 65% are boys. How many of the party are girls?

11. Train fares increase by $2\frac{1}{2}$%. What is the new price of a ticket which cost £18 before the increase?

12. There are 80 tins of soup on the shop shelf. $12\frac{1}{2}$% of them contain tomato soup. How many tins of tomato soup are there?

In the next exercise you will come across the following terms:

- **Profit:** This is the money you gain when you sell something for more than it costs you to make or buy.

- **Loss:** This is the money you lose when you sell something for less than it costs to make or buy.

- **Discount:** This is an amount by which the price of something is reduced, so the customer pays less.

Exercise 8.9: Problem solving (2)

1. Ian makes a table for £80
   He sells it, making a profit of 60%. How much money is his profit?

2. Disco Dave buys a DVD player for £180
   Since he pays with cash he is given a 5% discount. How much does he save by paying cash?

3. A bicycle is priced at £320
   Victoria is allowed 15% off the price (discount) of the bicycle as a prize for winning a cycle safety competition. How much does Victoria have to pay for the bicycle?

4. In a sale the price of everything is reduced (discounted) by 20%. By how much are the following reduced:

   (a) Jacket   priced at   £200

   (b) Trousers   £110

   (c) Shirt   £35

   (d) Belt   £4

5. Aston pays £7.50 for a model car and sells it to Martin, making a profit of 40%. How much does Martin pay for the car?

6. It costs a farmer £300 to produce a tonne of apples. Unfortunately he has to sell at a loss of 5%. How much does he sell a tonne of apples for?

7. A savings bank pays $2\frac{1}{2}\%$ interest per annum on deposits. Claudia deposits £5000
   How much interest will Claudia earn on this sum of money in a year?

8. Value Added Tax (VAT) is charged at a rate of $17\frac{1}{2}\%$ on the basic price. How much VAT is charged on

   (a) a radio   at basic price   £40

   (b) a fridge   £300

   (c) a lampshade   £28

   (d) a toothbrush   £1.60

Summary

Finding one quantity as a percentage of another

● Write quantities as a fraction using same units on top and bottom

● Multiply or divide top and bottom by the same number to make the bottom number 100

● Write the top number as a percentage

Examples:

What is 19 as a percentage of 50?

$\frac{19}{38} = \frac{38}{100}$ (multiply by 2)

19 is 38% of 50

Write 48 pence as a percentage of £3 (300p)

$\frac{48}{300} = \frac{16}{100}$ (divide by 3)

48 pence is 16% of £3

● 100% represents the **whole** amount.

● **Remember:** 50% = $\frac{1}{2}$ 25% = $\frac{1}{4}$ 75% = $\frac{3}{4}$

- 10% ($\frac{1}{10}$) is the base for many percentages.

To find 10% divide by 10

Examples:

    (i)   10% of 450 = 45

    (ii)   10% of 70 = 7

    (iii) 10% of 68 = 6.8

    (iv) 10% of 8   = 0.8

- To find multiples of 10%, first find 10%, then multiply.

Example:

Find 30% of 48

10% of 48 = 4.8

30% or 48 = 4.8 × 3

             = 14.4

- 5% and $2\frac{1}{2}$% are fractions of 10%.

Examples:

    (i)   Find 5% of 120

         10% of 120 = 12

         5% of 120 = 12 ÷ 2

                  = 6

    (ii)   Find $2\frac{1}{2}$% of 80

         10% of 80 = 8

         5% of 80   = 4   (8 ÷ 2)

         $2\frac{1}{2}$% of 80 = 2   (4 ÷ 2)

● Further percentages can be obtained by combining multiples and fractions of 10%.

Examples:

(i) $45\% = 40\%\ (10\% \times 4) + 5\%\ (\frac{1}{2}$ of 10%)

(ii) $72\frac{1}{2}\% = 70\%\ (10\% \times 7) + 2\frac{1}{2}\%\ (\frac{1}{2}$ of 5%)

● Value Added Tax (VAT) is usually charged at $17\frac{1}{2}\%$

$17\frac{1}{2}\% = 10\% + 5\% + 2\frac{1}{2}\%$

Example:

Find $17\frac{1}{2}\%$ of £72

$\quad$ 10% of £72 = £7.20

$+\quad$ 5% of £72 = £3.60 $\qquad (\frac{1}{2}$ of £7.20)

$+\quad$ $2\frac{1}{2}\%$ of £72 = £1.80 $\qquad (\frac{1}{2}$ of £3.60)

$\quad 17\frac{1}{2}\%$ of £72 = £12.60

Exercise 8.10: Summary exercise

Write the first quantity as a percentage of the second:

	First quantity	Second quantity
1.	7	20
2.	11p	25p
3.	30p	£5
4.	700 g	2 kg
5.	75 cm	2.5 m

Calculate:

6. 50% of 36

7. 50% of £5

8. 25% of 68

9. 25% of £12

10. 75% of 40

11. 75% of 92

12. 10% of 250

13. 10% of 70

14. 10% of 32

15. 10% of 6

16. 10% of £120

17. 10% of £38

18. 10% of £6

19. 10% of £0.70

20. 5% of 60

21. 5% of £40

22. 5% of £5

23. $2\frac{1}{2}$% of 120

24. $2\frac{1}{2}$% of £80

25. $2\frac{1}{2}$% of £24

26. 45% of 80

27. 85% of 240

28. 55% of £140

29. 35% of £18

30. 15% of £3.60

31. 65% of £4.80

32. $22\frac{1}{2}$% of 160

33. $32\frac{1}{2}$% of £56

34. $17\frac{1}{2}$% of £60

35. $17\frac{1}{2}$% of £36

36. Christine scores 50% in her maths test, which is marked out of 64 How many marks does she get?

37. 25% of the 112 patients in hospital arrived by ambulance. How many patients arrived by ambulance?

38. 75% of the loaves in a baker's van are white. If there are 96 loaves altogether how many white loaves are there?

39. For one day all prices are reduced by 10%. How much does Marcus save buying a jacket originally priced at £160?

40. A charge of 10% is added to the bill if a Chinese meal is delivered. How much is added if the meal costs £32.80?

41. 40% of the 65 biscuits in a tin are chocolate-covered. How many chocolate-covered biscuits are there?

42. 15% of the mass of a cherry cake are cherries. What is the mass of cherries in a cake that has a total mass of 500 grams?

43. A bowls club has 260 members of whom only 45% are aged under 60. How many members are aged over 60?

44. There are 1600 books in the school library of which $2\frac{1}{2}$% are books of poetry. How many books of poetry are there in the library?

45. Value Added Tax (VAT) is charged at 17.5% of the value of goods or services. How much VAT is charged on the following?

    (a) a bicycle valued at £360

    (b) a car service valued at £110

    (c) a kettle valued at £24

    (d) a dog lead valued at £7.60

End of chapter activity: Number crosses

These number crosses are made of two subtraction strips (the middle number in each strip is the same). The last number in each strip is made by subtracting the middle number from the first number.

Example:

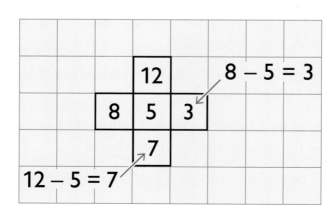

1. Copy and complete these number crosses.

Cross 1: 14 / 9 6 ▢ / ▢

Cross 2: 19 / 20 14 ▢ / ▢

Cross 3: 43 / 30 25 ▢ / ▢

Cross 4: ▢ / 7 3 / 9

Cross 5: ▢ / 40 6 / 17

Cross 6: 41 / ▢ 14 12

2. Write down any connection you notice between the first squares in the strips and the last squares in the strips.

Did you know?

- Your brain uses 20% of your body's energy, but it makes up only 2% of your body's weight.

- 89.06% of people normally write with their right hand, 10.6% with their left and 0.34% with either hand.

Chapter 9: Ratio and proportion

In this chapter we are going to look at **ratio**. A ratio shows how the different parts that make up a whole are related to each other. Here are some examples to show what this means.

Ratio

Examples:

(i)   In this necklace there are 2 white beads **for every** 1 red bead.

The ratio of white beads to red beads is 2 to 1

This is written as **2 : 1**

(ii)   Here there are 2 red beads **for every** 3 white beads.

The ratio of red beads to white beads is 2 to 3, or 2 : 3

Note: The order of the numbers must be the same as the order of the parts you are comparing.

In example (i):

white beads	:	red beads
2	:	1

In example (ii):

red beads	:	white beads
2	:	3

Like fractions, ratios should usually be written in their **lowest terms**. We divide both sides of the ratio by the same number until we can't divide any more.

Example:

Write the ratio of the number of red beads to the number of white beads

This necklace has 4 red beads **for every** 2 white beads.

The ratio of red beads : white beads is 4 : 2

We can divide both sides of the ratio by 2

4 : 2 = 2 : 1   (4 ÷ 2 = 2) and (2 ÷ 2 = 1)

The ratio of the number of red beads to the number of white beads is 2 : 1

Exercise 9.1: Basic ratio

Write the ratio of the number of red beads to the number of white beads.

Remember:
- Put the numbers in the correct order.
- Write the ratio in its lowest terms.

1.

2.

3.

4.

5.

6.

7.

8.

9.

10.

11.

12.

Quite often ratio questions are written as word problems.

Examples:

(i) There are 5 horses and 2 donkeys in a field. What is the ratio of the number of horses to the number of donkeys?

There are 5 horses to 2 donkeys so, the ratio of horses to donkeys is 5 : 2

(ii) There are 12 apples and 8 bananas in a fruit bowl.

(a) What is the ratio of apples to bananas?

Apples : bananas = 12 : 8

= 3 : 2   (Divide each side by 4 to get the answer in its lowest terms.)

(b) What is the ratio of bananas to apples?

The answer to part (a) tells us that there are 3 apples for every 2 bananas. We can turn this around and say that there are 2 bananas for every 3 apples.

Bananas : apples = 2 : 3

Exercise 9.2: Ratio problems

1. Basil has 5 pencils and 3 pens in his pencil case.
   (a) What is the ratio of pencils to pens?
   (b) What is the ratio of pens to pencils?

2. Ruby owns 2 necklaces and 7 bracelets.
   (a) What is the ratio of bracelets to necklaces?
   (b) What is the ratio of necklaces to bracelets?

3. Rufus owns 2 dogs and a cat.
   (a) What is the ratio of dogs to cats?
   (b) What is the ratio of cats to dogs?

4. There are 12 roses and 6 carnations in a bunch of flowers. How many roses are there for every carnation?

5. A box of biscuits contains 20 shortbread and 16 chocolate wafers.
   (a) What is the ratio of shortbread to chocolate wafers?
   (b) What is the ratio of chocolate wafers to shortbread?

6. Gary ate 14 bags of crisps and 6 packets of cheese biscuits last week. What is the ratio of the number of bags of crisps to the number of packets of cheese biscuits?

7. In June there were 20 sunny and 10 cloudy days. How many sunny days were there for every cloudy day?

8. At an 'egg and bacon' farm there are 10 pigs and 160 chickens. How many chickens are there for every pig?

9. There are 6 tables and 45 chairs in classroom 12A. What is the ratio of tables to chairs?

10. A packet of nuts contains 18 cashews and 16 almonds. How many cashews are there for every 8 almonds?

11. There are 21 boys and 35 girls in the gym club. What is the ratio of boys to girls?

12. Dan produces 30 hectares of wheat and 75 hectares of barley. What is the ratio of the number of hectares of wheat to the number of hectares of barley?

13. Each week Ken studies mathematics for 200 minutes and science for 180 minutes. What is the ratio of the time spent studying mathematics to the time spent studying science?

14. On Bank Holiday Monday Rico sells 360 ice creams and 120 ice lollies. How many ice creams did he sell for every ice lolly?

15. Membership of the Tennis Club costs £60 for adults and £24 for juniors. What is the ratio of the membership fee for adults compared to juniors?

16. Cook fries 5 eggs and 20 sausages. How many sausages are fried for every egg?

17. Bunter goes strawberry picking. He puts 60 strawberries in a bowl and eats 12
    How many strawberries does Bunter put in the bowl for every one that he eats?

18. The Village Hall is decorated with balloons. 30 are white, 60 are blue and 120 are red.
    (a) How many red balloons are there for every white balloon?
    (b) How many blue balloons are there for every white balloon?

19. Molly has been harvesting the fruit from the orchard. In her basket she has 6 apples, 9 pears and 12 plums.
    (a) What is the ratio of apples : pears
    (b) What is the ratio of apples : pears : plums?

20. There are 20 passengers sitting on a bus which has 56 seats. What is the ratio of occupied seats to empty seats?

Multiples of ratios

Let's use Brian the baker to demonstrate what we mean by multiples of a ratio.

Brian bakes white rolls and brown rolls in the ratio of 4 : 1

This tells us that Brian bakes 4 white rolls for every brown roll (remember, when describing a ratio we put the numbers in the same order as the items it compares).

Brian bakes many more than 5 rolls at a time. But however many he bakes, the ratio of 4 : 1 remains the same. The difference is that both sides of the ratio have been multiplied by the same number. For example:

4 : 1 = 8 : 2	(4 × **2** = 8 and 1 × **2** = 2)
= 12 : 3	(4 × **3** = 12 and 1 × **3** = 3)
= 16 : 4	(4 × **4** = 16 and 1 × **4** = 4)
= 400 : 100	(4 × **100** = 400 and 1 × **100** = 100)

If we are told how many white rolls Brian bakes, we can work out how many brown rolls he makes, and vice versa.

Example:

(i)   Brian bakes white rolls and brown rolls in the ratio of 4 : 1

   (a) If he bakes 24 white rolls, how many brown rolls does he bake?

      Set out your working as follows:

white	:	brown	
	:		(Write the ratio in words first.)
4	:	1	(Then write it in numbers. Make sure you put them in the right order.)
24	:	?	(You know that he bakes 24 white rolls, so write 24 in the 'white' column.)
24	:	6	(4 has been multiplied by 6 to make 24, so we must also multiply 1 by 6)

      Brian bakes 6 brown rolls.

(b) If he bakes 9 brown rolls, how many white rolls does he bake?

white : brown

4 : 1

? : 9   (Write 9 in the 'brown' column.)

36 : 9   (1 × 9 = 9 so work out 4 × 9 = 36)

Brian bakes 36 white rolls.

(ii) Boxes contain square biscuits and round biscuits in the ratio of 3 : 2

(a) A standard box contains 18 square biscuits. How many round biscuits are there?

square : round

3 : 2

18 : ?

18 : 12   (3 × 6 = 18 so work out 2 × 6 = 12)

There are 12 round biscuits.

(b) How many square biscuits are there in a large box which contains 16 round biscuits?

square : round

3 : 2

? : 16

24 : 16   (2 × 8 = 16 so work out 3 × 8 = 24)

There are 24 square biscuits.

Exercise 9.3: Multiples of ratios

1. Swigs Café sell bottles of lemonade and orangeade in the ratio of 3 : 1
    How many bottles of orangeade were sold yesterday if 30 bottles of lemonade were sold?

2. A father and his son's ages are in the ratio of 5 : 2
    How old is the son if the father is 50 years old?

3. The office manager buys 5 second class stamps for every 2 first class stamps. How many second class stamps are bought when she buys 12 first class stamps?

4. It takes 400 grams of flour to make 8 scones. How much flour is needed to make 24 scones?

5. A recipe for leek and potato soup for 4 people is as follows:

    800 *ml* vegetable stock
    300 grams leeks
    240 grams potatoes

    (a) Rewrite the recipe for 12 people.

    (b) What mass of potatoes is needed if there are 450 grams of leeks?

6. Pedro and his wife have a favourite recipe for chilli con carne which is enough to feed just them.

    It consists of:

    225 grams minced beef
    200 grams canned tomatoes
    110 grams kidney beans
    150 *ml* beef stock
    1 chilli

    (a) How much beef is needed for 6 people?

    (b) Tomatoes are sold in 500 gram cans. How many cans does Pedro need to buy to feed 9 people?

7. When mixed with water, 120 ml of concentrated juice produce 500 ml of grapefruit squash.
   (a) What quantity of squash is produced by 600 ml of concentrate?
   (b) How much concentrate is needed to produce 5 litres of squash?

8. Paula takes exercise by jogging for 10 minutes followed by walking for 3 minutes. For how long does she jog if she spends 15 minutes walking?

9. Strawberries and raspberries are combined in the ratio of 8 : 7 to make a special summer fruit mixture. What mass of strawberries is needed to mix with 56 grams of raspberries?

10. The stationery company Classroom Needs makes pens and pencils in the ratio of 5 : 12
    How many pens are made for every 144 pencils?

11. The length and width of a rectangle are in the ratio of 3 : 2
    (a) How wide is the rectangle if it is 12 cm long?
    (b) What is the rectangle's length if it is 12 cm wide?

12. To make 500 grams of butterscotch Poppy needs
    500 grams demerara sugar
    170 ml water
    50 grams butter
    (a) Rewrite the recipe for 250 grams of butterscotch.
    (b) Poppy has 1 kg of butter and as much sugar and water as she wants. What is the largest amount of butterscotch that she can make?

13. A Palm Special is made with:
    60 ml fresh orange juice
    40 ml coconut milk
    100 grams ice

    A party of 4 each order a Palm Special.
    (a) How much orange juice is needed?
    (b) The barman has only $\frac{1}{2}$ a litre of coconut milk left but plenty of orange juice and ice. What is the maximum number of Palm Specials that he can make?

14. A 35 gram packet of powder will, when mixed with milk, make 300 ml of bread sauce.

   (a) How many packets are needed to make 3 litres of sauce?

   (b) How much sauce can be made with 140 grams of powder?

15. 2 baguettes are enough to feed 5 children.

   (a) How many children will 12 baguettes feed?

   (b) How many baguettes must be bought to feed 40 children?

16. The basic ingredients of a 250 gram jar of pickle are

   > 120 grams cauliflower
   > 70 grams onion
   > 40 grams apple
   > 20 grams carrot

   (a) What size of jar contains 100 grams of apple?

   (b) How much cauliflower is there in a kilogram jar?

17. Chef looks up a recipe for fish pie to feed 4:

   > 750 grams potatoes
   > 350 grams white fish
   > 300 ml milk

   (a) Rewrite the recipe for 6 people.

   (b) A pie contains 1.2 litres of milk. How many people was this pie made for?

18. There are 2 tokens on packets of Grow Well packets of fertilizer. A rose bush is given free in exchange for 5 tokens.

   (a) George has 12 tokens. How many rose bushes will he get?

   (b) Mrs Potter wants to get 4 rose bushes. What is the least number of packets that she must buy?

19. Gallons and litres are in the ratio of 2 : 9

   (a) How many gallons are there in a 36 litre barrel?

   (b) An empty oil tank has a capacity of 100 gallons.
      How many litres of oil are needed to fill the tank?

20. There are 11 pounds for every 5 kilograms.

    (a) An airline baggage allowance is 33 pounds.

    What is this allowance in kilograms?

    (b) What is George's mass in pounds if he weighs in at 120 kilograms?

Total of ratios

Sam has a packet of red and green jellies. He knows two things:

● the jellies are in the ratio, red : green of 3 : 2

● there are 12 red jellies in the packet

Does he have enough information to work out the **total** number of jellies in the packet?

Yes, he does.

3 has been multiplied by 4 to make 12 (red jellies)

So there are 2 × 4 = 8 green jellies

So there are 12 + 8 = 20 jellies in the packet in total.

Exercise 9.4: Total of ratios

1. A box of chocolates is made up of crème and hard centres in the ratio of 7 : 4
   How many chocolates are there altogether if there are 28 with crème centres?

2. Men and women members of a darts club are in the ratio of 8 : 3
   If there are 32 men, what is the total number of members?

3. Blurp is a shade of paint made when blue and purple paint are mixed in the ratio of 5 : 3
   How many litres of Blurp are produced when 9 litres of purple paint are used?

4. Alan is 11 years old and Sue is 9 years old. They win a prize in a raffle and share the prize in the ratio of their ages. How much is the prize if Alan's share is £55?

5. Karim divides his herd of camels between his sons, Ahmed and Mustapha in the ratio of 4 : 3
How many camels are there in the herd if Ahmed's share is 120?

Proportion

Proportion is another word that can be used to describe mathematical situations. Proportion shows how one part, or type of part, is related to the whole, or total number of parts. Here is an example to show what this means.

If there are 5 red biros and 3 blue biros (total 8 biros)
● the proportion of red biros is 5 out of 8
● the proportion of blue biros is 3 out of 8

It is important to understand the difference between **ratio** and **proportion**.

In this example, the **ratio** of red to blue biros is 5 : 3, meaning 5 red biros **for** every 3 blue biros.

the **proportion** of red biros is 5 out of 8, meaning 5 red biros **in** every 8 biros.

We usually write a proportion as a fraction.
So we can say:

5 out of the 8 biros are red; or

$\frac{5}{8}$ of the biros are red.

Example:

There are 15 girls and 9 boys in an orchestra. What proportion of the orchestra is girls?

Proportion of girls in the orchestra = 15 out of total orchestra

$\qquad\qquad\qquad\qquad\quad$ = 15 out of 24 $\qquad$ (15 + 9)

$\qquad\qquad\qquad\qquad\quad$ = 5 out of 8 $\qquad$ (÷3 to get lowest terms)

$\qquad\qquad\qquad\qquad\quad$ = $\frac{5}{8}$

Exercise 9.5: Proportion

Remember to give your answer in lowest terms when necessary.

1. There are 12 red and 5 blue exercise books on the desk. What proportion of the books is red?

2. A basket contains 14 hens' eggs and 4 duck eggs. What proportion of the eggs is duck eggs?

3. A box of biscuits has 10 chocolate and 20 plain biscuits in it. What proportion of the biscuits is chocolate?

4. 12 children buy banana milk-shakes and 8 buy strawberry milk-shakes. What proportion of the children buys a strawberry milk-shake?

5. Adam buys 120 daffodil bulbs and 80 tulip bulbs. What proportion of the total is tulip bulbs?

6. Gunpowder contains saltpetre and sulphur in the ratio of 6 : 1
    What proportion is saltpetre?

7. Mortar is made of a mixture of sand and cement in the ratio of 3 : 1
    What proportion of a load of mortar is cement?

8. The fruit basis of Sunrise Crush is made of oranges and lemons in the ratio of 5 : 2
    What proportion of the fruit is lemons?

9. A newsagent sells 40 copies of *Moon* for every 5 copies of *The Viewer*. What proportion of his sales is copies of *Moon*?

10. The catering manager orders 1 tin of marmalade for every 5 tins of jam. How many tins of marmalade will there be in a total order of 12 tins?

Summary

Ratio

A **ratio** shows how parts of a whole are related (connected).

Remember:

- The order of the words and the order of the numbers are kept the same.

- Ratios are usually written in their lowest terms.

- To keep ratios the same, each part of the ratio must be multiplied/divided by the same number.

- The sum of the ratios gives the total number of items.

Examples:

(i)

There is 1 purple bead **for every** 3 white beads.

purple	:	white		white	:	purple
1	:	3		3	:	1

(ii)

There are 6 purple beads **for every** 4 white beads

purple	:	white		white	:	purple	
6	:	4		4	:	6	(Divide by 2 to get lowest terms.)
3	:	2		2	:	3	

(iii) Children eat apple crumble and rice pudding in the ratio of 7 : 3

How many children eat rice pudding when 28 have apple crumble?

apple crumble	:	rice pudding	
7	:	3	
28	:	12	($7 \times 4 = 28$ and $3 \times 4 = 12$)

12 children eat rice pudding.

(iv) At break all the staff drink either tea or coffee in the ratio of 5 : 4

How many staff are there if 12 drink coffee?

tea	:	coffee	
5	:	4	(coffee $4 \times 3 = 12$
15	:	12	tea $5 \times 3 = 15$)

There are 27 (15 + 12) members of staff.

Proportion

Proportion shows how one part relates to the whole.

Remember:

- Add the parts together to find the value of the whole.
- Write the proportion as a fraction.

Examples:

(i) There are 10 English cheeses and 6 French cheeses on the market stall.

What proportion of the cheeses is French?

Proportion of cheese is French = 6 out of total

$$= 6 \text{ out of } 16 \quad (10 + 6 = 16)$$
$$= 3 \text{ out of } 8 \quad (\div 2)$$

There are 3 French cheeses **in every** 8 cheeses; or

$\frac{3}{8}$ of the cheeses are French.

Exercise 9.6: Summary exercise

1. Write down the ratio of the number of ticks (✓) to the number of crosses (✗).

(a) | ✓ | ✓ | ✓ | ✗ | ✗ | ✓ | ✓ | ✓ | ✗ | ✗ | ✓ | ✓ | ✓ | ✗ | ✗ |

(b) | ✗ | ✓ | ✓ | ✓ | ✓ | ✗ | ✓ | ✓ | ✓ | ✓ | ✗ | ✓ | ✓ | ✓ | ✓ |

(c) | ✓ | ✓ | ✓ | ✓ | ✗ | ✗ | ✓ | ✓ | ✓ | ✓ | ✗ | ✗ |

(d) | ✗ | ✗ | ✗ | ✓ | ✓ | ✓ | ✓ | ✓ | ✓ | ✗ | ✗ | ✗ | ✓ | ✓ | ✓ | ✓ | ✓ | ✓ |

2. There are 18 apple trees and 8 plum trees in William's garden. What is the ratio of apple trees to plum trees?

3. The Ladies' Cookery Circle makes pots of jam and honey in the ratio of 7 : 2
   How many pots of honey are there if 35 pots of jam are made?

4. A group of students do well in their exams. A grades and B grades are gained in the ratio of 5 : 3
   36 B grades are gained. How many A grades are there?

5. The members of a rackets club choose to play either tennis or squash in the ratio of 11 : 8
   How many members are there if 24 play squash?

6. You are told that 2 inches are the equivalent of 5 centimetres.

   (a) Yves is 72 inches tall. What is his height in centimetres?

   (b) A snake is 40 centimetres long. Write this length in inches.

7. Anton makes a delicious mushroom soup. His recipe for 4 is:

   1200 ml vegetable stock
   600 ml milk
   400 grams mushrooms

   (a) Rewrite the recipe for 10 people.

   Anton has gathered 1.2 kg of mushrooms. He has a large quantity of stock and milk.

   (b) What is the largest number to whom he can give soup?

8. Monique found an old recipe for lamb stew to feed 4 people:

   900 grams lamb shank
   3 onions
   300 ml lamb stock
   150 ml white wine

   (a) How many onions are needed to make a stew for 20 people?

   (b) What is the largest number that can be fed if she has 4.5 kg of lamb?

9. Abdul makes a special blend of coffee. He mixes 100 grams of Columbian with 150 grams of Mocha.

    (a) How much Columbian does he mix with 750 grams of Mocha?

    (b) How much Mocha is there in a kilogram jar of coffee?

10. A spice merchant mixes 20 grams of white pepper with 30 grams of black pepper.

    (a) How much black pepper is there in 500 grams of mixture?

    (b) What is the mass of a bag of the mixture which contains 100 grams of white pepper?

11. A channel ferry has space for 4 cars for every lorry.

    (a) How many lorries are there if 140 cars are being carried?

    (b) How many cars are there when there are 420 vehicles altogether?

12. Adam and Eve share an apple in the ratio of 2 : 1
    What proportion of the apple does Adam eat?

13. On Monday the secretary sends 20 letters by 1st class post and 35 by 2nd class.

    (a) (i) What is the ratio of the number of letters sent 1st class to the number of those sent 2nd class?

    (ii) What proportion of the letters are sent 1st class?

    On Tuesday she sends letters by 1st and 2nd class post in the same ratio as on Monday but only 12 letters are sent 1st class.

    (b) (i) How many letters are sent 2nd class?

    (ii) How many letters altogether are posted on Tuesday?

End of chapter activity: Tricky triangles

Here are some patterns made of dots.

Pattern 1   **Pattern 2**   **Pattern 3**   **Pattern 4**

1. Draw the next four patterns.

2. Copy and complete the table for patterns 5 to 8

Pattern number	Number of dots	Pattern number × next pattern number
1	1	1 × 2 = 2
2	3	2 × 3 = 6
3	6	3 × 4 = 12
4	10	4 × 5 = 20
5		
6		
7		
8		
9		
10		

3. Can you see a relationship between the numbers in the last two columns?

   Use it to complete the final two rows of the table.

   The numbers in the second column are called the **triangle numbers**. This is because they can be drawn as triangles.

   We can also make the triangle numbers by adding **consecutive** whole numbers. (Consecutive means 'following on from each other'.) You can see that this works by looking at the number of dots in each row of the patterns you have drawn.

4. Continue the pattern below up to the 10th triangle number.

$$1 = 1$$
$$3 = 1 + 2$$
$$6 = 1 + 2 + 3$$
$$10 = 1 + 2 + 3 + 4$$

5. Use what you have learnt to answer these questions.

   (a) What is the 15th triangle number?

   (b) What is the sum of all the numbers from 1 to 50?

   (c) What is the sum of all the numbers from 1 to 100?

   (d) What is the sum of all the numbers from 21 to 40?

Did you know?

A 'jiffy' is an actual unit of time. It means $\frac{1}{1000}$th of a second.

Chapter 10: Functions

A **function** is like a machine that gives you instructions about what to do with a number. We put a number in (the **input**), perform the function, and get another number out (the **output**).

Sometimes there is more that one function that needs to be performed in order to find the output number. In such cases we work from left to right through the functions.

Examples:

	Input	→	Function	→	Output	
Single function	8	→	× 3	→	24	(8 × 3 = 24)
Double function	15	→	× 2, ÷ 3	→	10	(First 15 × 2 = 30, then 30 ÷ 3 = 10)
Double function	10	→	÷ 5, − 3	→	⁻1	(First 10 ÷ 5 = 2, then 2 − 3 = ⁻1)

Exercise 10.1: Finding outputs

Find the output for each of the following functions:

	Input		Function		Output
	Input		**Function**		**Output**
1.	16	→	+ 7	→	?
2.	7	→	− 10	→	?
3.	6	→	× 12	→	?
4.	36	→	÷ 9	→	?
5.	13	→	− 3, ÷ 2	→	?
6.	8	→	+ 2, × 3	→	?

	Input	Function	Output
7.	45	→ ÷ 9, + 7 →	?
8.	20	→ × 4, − 13 →	?

9. Think of 30, divide by 5 and then add 10

10. Think of 30, add 10 and then divide by 5

Inverse functions

In the section above we were given the **input**. To find the **output** we worked through the functions (if there was more than one) from **left to right**.

If we are given the **output**, we can find the **input** by working backwards, using the **inverse functions**.

If there is more than one function, we must work from **right to left**.

    + is the inverse of −

    − is the inverse of +

    × is the inverse of ÷

    ÷ is the inverse of ×

Note: You have to work out the **inverse** function because only the function is given.

Examples:

	Input	←	Function	←	Output
Single function	18	←	÷ 3	←	6
	(6 × 3 = 18)		(The inverse of ÷ 3 is × 3)		(Start here) 👉
Double function	15	←	− 7, × 3	←	24
	(First 24 ÷ 3 = 8)		(The inverse of × 3 is ÷ 3)		(Remember to work from
	(Then 8 + 7 = 15)		(The inverse of − 7 is + 7)		right to left.) 👉
	Input	←	**Function**	←	**Output**

Always check your answer by using it as the input and working through the function to find the output. Check that it is the same output you started with.

In the examples above:

$18 \div 3 = 6$ ✓

$15 - 7 = 8$ then $8 \times 3 = 24$ ✓

Exercise 10.2: Finding inputs

Find the input in each of the following functions:

	Input		Function		Output
1.	?	←	+ 7	←	24
2.	?	←	− 9	←	18
3.	?	←	× 6	←	6
4.	?	←	÷ 5	←	20
5.	?	←	+ 3, − 4	←	17
6.	?	←	× 4, + 3	←	43
7.	?	←	+ 3, ÷ 4	←	10
8.	?	←	− 4, + 3	←	28
9.	?	←	× 3, − 4	←	23
10.	?	←	− 4, ÷ 3	←	5
11.	?	←	× 5, + 2	←	37
12.	?	←	− 2, ÷ 5	←	20
13.	?	←	× 5, − 2	←	48
14.	?	←	÷ 2, × 5	←	45
15.	?	←	− 2, ÷ 3	←	15
16.	?	←	÷ 3, − 2	←	15

	Input		Function		Output
17.	?	←	× 3, + 2	←	32
18.	?	←	+ 2, × 3	←	30
19.	?	←	× 2, ÷ 4	←	60
20.	?	←	÷ 2, × 4	←	60

Function puzzles

This puzzle is also a function, but it is written in words.

Imagine a conversation between Louis and India:

Louis: 'Think of a number, subtract 10 and then multiply by 6.'

India thinks of a number in her head, subtracts 10 and then multiplies by 6

Louis: 'What is your answer?'

India: '18'

Louis: 'Let me guess the number you thought of was 13'

India: 'Yes, but how do you know?'

This isn't a trick, all Louis has done is to take India's answer (the output) and worked through the inverse functions (÷ 6 and then + 10) to find the input. This is just what we did in the last exercise.

Input	←	Function	←	Output
13	←	− 10, × 6	←	18

(18 ÷ 6 = 3 and 3 + 10 = 13)

Check: 13 − 10 = 3 and 3 × 6 = 18 ✓

Try this out on your friends.

Exercise 10.3: Function puzzles

What number do you think of if you:

1. add 2, subtract 6 and get 3?

2. add 3, multiply by 4 and get 32?

3. add 1, divide by 7 and get 2?

4. subtract 4, add 5 and get 10?

5. subtract 2, multiply by 3 and get 30?

6. subtract 7, divide by 9 and get 2?

7. multiply by 5, add 2 and get 32?

8. multiply by 2, subtract 1 and get 15?

9. multiply by 6, divide by 3 and get 20?

10. divide by 7, add 2 and get 5?

11. divide by 8, subtract 4 and get 0?

12. divide by 2, multiply by 3 and get 18?

13. add 2, halve the answer and get 12?

14. halve it, add 2 and get 12?

15. add 2, multiply by 4, divide by 5 and get 20?

End of chapter activity: Building bricks

A child's building bricks are arranged in layers.

Each layer has 2 more bricks than the layer above.

1. Draw the patterns for 4 layers and 5 layers

2. Complete the table

1 layer   2 layers   3 layers

Number of layers		Total number of bricks
1	1	1
2	1 + 3	4
3	1 + 3 + 5	
4		
5		

3. Now answer these questions about the numbers in the table.

(a) Describe in as much detail as possible what kind of numbers are added together to get the total number of bricks.

(b) What kind of numbers are in the third column?

(c) How many bricks will there be in
   (i) 8 layers?
   (ii) 30 layers?

(d) How many layers can Hugh arrange with 100 bricks?

(e) How many extra layers can Hugh arrange with another 100 bricks?

Did you know?

'99' is not just the name of an ice cream cornet with a flake.

Look at this pattern:

99 × 11 = 1089
99 × 22 = 2178
99 × 33 = 3267
99 × 44 = 4356
99 × 55 = 5445

Copy and complete the next few calculations in the series:

99 × 66 =
99 × 77 =
99 × 88 =
99 × 99 =

What do you notice about your first and last answers?

Chapter 11: Inequalities

We are very familiar with the word **equal** and its sign **=**. We use this term when the values either side of the equals sign are the same or equal.

Numbers that are not equal to each other can be **compared** to each other by using special signs:

> means **is larger/greater than**.

Example:	6 > 2	means 6 is larger than 2
	$n > 2$	means the value of n is larger than 2

< means **is smaller/less than**.

Example:	1 < 3	means 1 is smaller than 3
	$n < 3$	means the value of n is less than 3

There are also two other signs that we can use to compare numbers:

≥ means **is larger than or equal to**.

Example:	$n \geq 6$	means the value of n is either equal to 6 or larger than 6
		For example, n could be 6, 7.5 or 13 (these are just a few of many possibilities).

≤ means **is less than or equal to**.

Example:	$n \leq 3$	means the value of n is either equal to 3 or smaller than 3
		For example, n could be ⁻2, 0 or 3 (amongst many other possibilities).

All these signs are known as **signs of inequality**.

Exercise 11.1: Inequalities

Write these number comparisons using the correct symbols:

1. 10 is greater than 6

2. 30 is larger than 29

3. 6 is smaller than 8

4. 4 is less than n

5. −2 is less than 0

6. n is less than or equal to 8

7. n is smaller than or equal to 0

8. n is greater than or equal to 65

9. n is greater than or equal to 5

10. n is larger than or equal to 4

Finding largest and smallest whole number (integral) values

From these comparisons of n we can often work out some of the possible values of n.

Here are some examples (all answers will be whole numbers):

Examples:

(i)   What is the largest value of n when $n < 4$?

   n has to be less than 4, and the next smallest whole number below 4 is 3

   The largest possible value of n is 3

(ii) What is the largest value of n when $n \leq 4$?

   n can be less than or equal to 4 so the largest number n could be is 4

   The largest possible value of n is 4

(iii) What is the smallest value of n when $n > 7$?

n must be greater than 7, and the smallest whole number after 7 is 8

The smallest possible value of n is 8

(iv) What is the smallest value of n when $n \geq 7$?

n can be greater than or equal to 7 so the smallest number n could be is 7

The smallest possible value of n is 7

When negative numbers are involved, remember which way you are going on the number line.

Here's one to remind you:

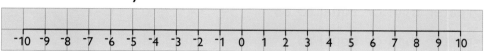

Examples:

(i) $^-4 < ^-3$

(ii) $^-1 < 0$

(iii) $6 > 3$

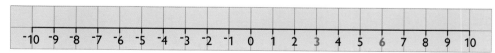

(iv) $4 > ^-1$

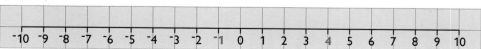

(v)   What is the largest value of n when $n < ^-3$?
Answer: $^-4$

(vi)   What is the smallest value of n when $n > ^-6$?
Answer: $^-5$

Exercise 11.2: Finding largest and smallest whole number (integral) values

Write down the largest whole number (integral) value of n when:

1. $n < 9$

2. $n \leq 7$

3. $n < {}^-5$

4. $n \leq {}^-3$

5. $n < 0$

Write down the smallest whole number (integral) value of n when:

6. $n > 6$

7. $n \geq 10$

8. $n > {}^-4$

9. $n \geq {}^-4$

10. $n > 0$

Range of values

Signs of inequality can be used to show the limits of a range of values.

Examples:

(i) Write down all the possible whole number values of n when $3 < n < 7$

n is larger than 3 but less than 7

We can show this on a number line.

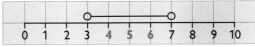

$n = 4, 5$ or 6

(ii) Write down all the possible whole number values of n when $8 > n \geq 5$

n is less than 8 but greater than or equal to 5

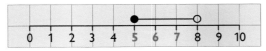

The circle above 5 is filled in to show that 5 is included in the answer.

$n = 5, 6$ or 7

Exercise 11.3: Range of values

Write down all the possible whole number (integral) values of n. You can use a number line to help you.

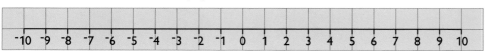

1.	$1 < n < 5$	6.	$8 < n \leq 10$
2.	$7 \leq n < 10$	7.	$8 \leq n \leq 10$
3.	$5 < n \leq 8$	8.	$^-4 < n < ^-1$
4.	$8 < n < 10$	9.	$^-4 < n \leq ^-1$
5.	$8 \leq n < 10$	10.	$^-4 \leq n < ^-1$

11.	$^-4 \leq n \leq ^-1$	16.	$11 > n > 6$
12.	$2 < n \leq 6$	17.	$8 \geq n > 5$
13.	$^-3 \leq n < 0$	18.	$4 > n \geq 2$
14.	$^-1 < n < 2$	19.	$9 > n > 7$
15.	$0 \leq n \leq 4$	20.	$9 > n \geq 7$

21.	$9 \geq n > 7$	26.	$5 \geq n \geq ^-2$
22.	$9 \geq n \geq 7$	27.	$^-1 > n > ^-4$
23.	$5 > n > ^-2$	28.	$^-5 \geq n \geq ^-8$
24.	$5 > n \geq ^-2$	29.	$0 \geq n > ^-3$
25.	$5 \geq n > ^-2$	30.	$7 > n > 0$

31.	$8 < n < 12$	36.	$4 \leq n < 5$
32.	$9 > n > 4$	37.	$^-7 < n < ^-3$
33.	$^-4 < n < ^-1$	38.	$0 \geq n \geq ^-4$
34.	$^-6 > n > ^-9$	39.	$^-2 < n < 2$
35.	$3 \geq n > ^-1$	40.	$2 > n > ^-2$

End of chapter activity: How many triangles?

These patterns are made up of small triangles.

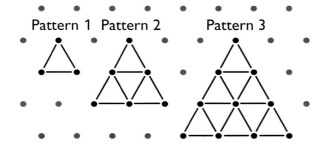

Pattern 1 Pattern 2   Pattern 3

1. Draw patterns 4 and 5

2. Copy and complete the table.

Pattern number	Number of small triangles	Number of dots
1	1	3
2	4	6
3	9	10
4		
5		

3. Answer these questions about the patterns.
   (a) What is the name for the numbers in the second column?
   (b) What is the name for the numbers in the third column?
   (c) How many dots are there in pattern 8?
   (d) How many small triangles are there in pattern 9?
   (e) Which pattern has 144 small triangles?

Did you know?

Nines again!

$999\ 999 \times 2 = 1\ 999\ 998$
$999\ 999 \times 3 = 2\ 999\ 997$
$999\ 999 \times 4 = 3\ 999\ 996$
$999\ 999 \times 5 = 4\ 999\ 995$
$999\ 999 \times 6 = 5\ 999\ 994$

Copy and complete the next few calculations in the sequence:

$999\ 999 \times 7 =$
$999\ 999 \times 8 =$
$999\ 999 \times 9 =$
$999\ 999 \times 10 =$

Chapter 12: Decimal multiplication

We have already multiplied decimals when working out answers to problems involving money. In this chapter we are going to look further at multiplications involving decimals.

It is useful to remind ourselves of place values before we start.

| Hundreds | Tens | Units | • | tenths | hundredths | thousandths |

So, for example, 7.35 is 7 **Units**, 3 **tenths** and 5 **hundredths**.

22.05 is 2 **Tens**, 2 **Units**, 0 **tenths** and 5 **hundredths**

Always set out your calculations carefully.

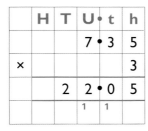

Examples:

(i)   7.35 × 3 is the same as £7.35 × 3

Here we are going to use the formal method of calculation, using carrying.

H	T	U	•	t	h
		7	•	3	5
×					3
	2	2	•	0	5
			₁	₁	

(**Step 1:** 5 × 3 = 15 so write 5 in the answer row and carry 1)

(**Step 2:** 3 × 3 = 9, plus the carried 1 is 10, so write 0 in the answer row and carry 1)

(**Step 3:** 7 × 3 = 21, plus the carried 1 is 22)

(Remember to carry the decimal point down into your answer row.)

(ii)   0.86 × 4 is the same as £0.86 × 4

H	T	U	•	t	h
		0	•	8	6
×					4
		3	•	4	4
			₂		

(iii) 8.5 × 7 is the same as £8.50 × 7

H	T	U	•	t	h
		8	•	5	(0)
×					7
5	9	•	5	(0)
		3			

(8.5 is the same as 8.50)

(Remember, the first step is 0 × 7 = 0)

Tip: When multiplying, we expect to get larger numbers. If the question involves **Units**, the answer is likely to involve **Tens** and **Units**. If the question involves **Tens** and **Units**, the answer is likely to involve **Hundreds**, **Tens** and **Units**. Therefore when you set out your frame you will need to add one more column to the left.

Exercise 12.1: Multiplying by a single integer

Calculate:

1. 5.6 × 2

2. 2.8 × 3

3. 7.9 × 4

4. 8.7 × 5

5. 3.4 × 6

6. 0.21 × 7

7. 0.72 × 8

8. 0.83 × 9

9. 2.83 × 2

10. 7.96 × 3

11. 1.74 × 4

12. 3.97 × 5

13. 2.79 × 6

14. 18.6 × 7

15. 75.4 × 8

16. 49.7 × 9

17. 14.8 × 6

18. 56.3 × 4

19. 9.05 × 7

20. 70.8 × 3

Multiplication of decimals by 10, 100 and 1000

When we multiply decimals by 10, 100 and 1000 we follow exactly the same rules as we do when we are working with whole numbers:

When we **multiply by 10**, the digits move **1 place to the left**.

Th	H	T	U•	t	h	th
			2•	7	3	
		2	7•	3		

(2.73 × 10)

When we **multiply by 100**, the digits move **2 places to the left**.

Th	H	T	U•	t	h	th
			2•	7	3	
	2	7	3			

(2.73 × 100)

When we **multiply by 1000**, the digits move **3 places to the left**.

Th	H	T	U•	t	h	th
			2•	7	3	
2	7	3	0			

(2.73 × 1000)

Exercise 12.2: Mulitiplication of decimals by 10, 100 and 1000

Calculate the following:

1. 4.12 × 10
2. 3.56 × 100
3. 3.56 × 1000

4. 23.45 × 10
5. 45.12 × 100
6. 12.34 × 1000

7. 123.15 × 10
8. 573.02 × 100
9. 482.20 × 1000

Multiplication of decimals by multiples of 10, 100 and 1000

Knowing how to multiply decimals by 10, 100 and 1000 will help us to multiply by multiples of 10, 100 and 1000

For example, we can multiply by numbers such as 30, 200, 4000 by using factors.

Examples:

(i) Calculate 2.73×30

We can think of 30 as 3×10

$2.73 \times 10 = 27.3$ (**Step 1:** Multiply the decimal by the 10 first.)

$27.3 \times 3 = 81.9$ (**Step 2:** Then multiply by 3 You may find it easier to set this out as a formal calculation.)

	2	7	·	3
×				3
	8	1	·	9
	2			

$2.73 \times 30 = 81.9$

(ii) Calculate 17.9×60

We can think of 60 as 6×10

$17.9 \times 10 = 179$

$179 \times 6 = 1074$

		1	7	9
×				6
	1	0	7	4
		4	5	

$17.9 \times 60 = 1074$

(iii)   Calculate 0.183 × 200

We can think of 200 as 2 × 100

0.183 × 100 = 18.3

18.3 × 2 = 36.6

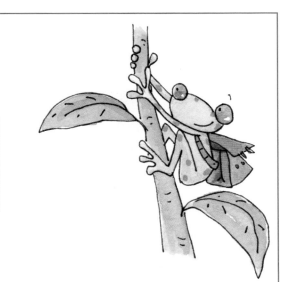

	1	8 · 3
×		2
	3	6 · 6
1		

0.183 × 200 = 36.6

(iv)   Calculate 1.37 × 400

We can think of 400 as 4 × 100

1.37 × 100 = 137

137 × 4 = 548

	1	3	7
×			4
	5	4	8
	1	2	

1.37 × 400 = 548

(v)   Calculate 21.8 × 700

We can think of 700 as 7 × 100

21.8 × 100 = 2180

2180 × 7 = 15 260

		2	1	8	0
×					7
	1	5	2	6	0
		1	5		

21.8 × 700 = 15 260

(vi) Calculate 0.0371 × 4000

We can think of 4000 as 4 × 1000

0.0371 × 1000 = 37.1

37.1 × 4 = 148.4

			3	7 · 1
×				4
	1	4	8 · 4
		2		

0.0371 × 4000 = 148.4

(vii) Calculate 1.46 × 7000

We can think of 7000 as 7 × 1000

1.46 × 1000 = 1460

1460 × 7 = 10 220

		1	4	6	0
×					7
	1	0	2	2	0
		3	4		

1.46 × 7000 = 10 220

Exercise 12.3: Multiplication of decimals by multiples of 10, 100 and 1000

Calculate:

1. 3.2 × 20
2. 4.7 × 60
3. 0.19 × 30
4. 3.25 × 70
5. 1.39 × 50
6. 1.09 × 40
7. 0.148 × 80
8. 23.6 × 90
9. 14.7 × 60
10. 0.027 × 50

11. 8.37 × 400

12. 1.46 × 300

13. 7.43 × 500

14. 0.453 × 300

15. 0.087 × 900

16. 8.4 × 700

17. 0.138 × 3000

18. 1.86 × 5000

19. 14.3 × 4000

20. 3.6 × 6000

Multiplying a decimal by a decimal

So far you have always multiplied decimals by an integer (whole number).

We will now see what happens when you multiply two decimals together.

Examples:

(i)　Calculate 3.8 × 0.6

Step 1: First, ignore the decimal points and multiply the numbers.

		3	8
×			6
	2	2	8
		4	

Step 2: Now the decimal point must be replaced.

38 is 10 times larger than 3.8

6 is 10 times larger than 0.6

This means that the answer (228) is 100 (10 × 10) times larger than it should be. We must make it 100 times smaller by dividing by 100

Note: When we divide by 100, the digits move 2 places to the right.

228 ÷ 100 = 2.28

So, 3.8 × 0.6 = 2.28

(ii) Calculate 4.78 × 0.4

Step 1:

		4	7	8
×				4
	1	9	1	2
		3	3	

Step 2: 478 is 100 times larger than 4.78

4 is 10 times larger than 0.4

We must divide 1912 by 1000 (100 × 10).

1912 ÷ 100 = 1.912

So, 4.78 × 0.4 = 1.912

Simple method

You will be pleased to know that there is a very simple method to help you place the decimal point correctly in the answer:

The number of decimal places in the answer is the same as the number of decimal places in the question.

Look at the examples above

(i) **3.8 × 0.6** (2 numbers after the decimal points) = 2.**28** (2 numbers after the decimal point)

(ii) **4.78 × 0.4** (3 numbers after the decimal points) = 1.**912** (3 numbers after the decimal point)

So, to multiply a decimal by a decimal, follow these steps:

Step 1: Multiply the numbers, ignoring the decimal point.

Step 2: Count the number of decimal places in the question (look at both numbers).

Step 3: Put the same number of decimal places in the answer.

Examples:

(i) Calculate 9.8 × 0.7

Step 1:

		9	8
×			7
	6	8	6
		5	

Step 2: There are two decimal places in the question.

Step 3: Put the decimal point in, to give 6.86

9.8 × 0.7 = 6.86

(ii) Calculate 2.67 × 0.09

Step 1:

	2	6	7
×			9
2	4	0	3
	6	6	

Step 2: There are four decimal places in the question.

Step 3: Put the decimal point in, to give 0.2403

2.67 × 0.09 = 0.2403

(iii) Calculate 1.74 × 0.04

Step 1:

1	7	4
×		4
6	9	6
2	1	

Step 2: There are four decimal places in the question.

Step 3: Put the decimal point in, to give 0.0696 (Note the extra 0 to give the 4 decimal places.)

1.74 × 0.04 = 0.0696

Exercise 12.4: Multiplying a decimal by a decimal

Calculate:

1. 7.8 × 0.4
2. 9.3 × 0.5
3. 12.5 × 0.3
4. 48.7 × 0.6
5. 5.34 × 0.9

6. 2.84 × 0.7
7. 75.8 × 0.08
8. 45.3 × 0.03
9. 1.6 × 0.4
10. 3.25 × 0.3

11. 18.3 × 0.05
12. 142 × 0.004
13. 3.2 × 0.3
14. 1.4 × 0.05
15. 0.23 × 0.08

16. 0.021 × 0.4
17. 1.41 × 0.0003
18. 6.7 × 0.5
19. 74.8 × 0.9
20. 2.87 × 0.07

Decimal numbers in word problems are often measures. Make sure that you include the units in your answers.

Exercise 12.5: Problem solving

1. Graham buys six model cars which cost £5.65 each. How much does he pay altogether?

2. A fencing panel is 1.90 metres long. What is the total length of seven panels placed end to end?

3. In a box there are eight fruit cakes, each with mass 1.75 kilograms. What is the total mass of the cakes?

4. Cans have a capacity of 0.330 litre. What is the capacity of five such cans?

5. At a gymnastics competition four judges each give Leon Voltski 9.355 points. What is the total of points given?

6. Lead has a mass of 11.4 grams per cubic centimetre (cm³). Simon uses a 3 cm³ lead weight when fishing. What is the mass of Simon's weight?

7. 1 inch = 2.54 centimetres. How many centimetres are equal to 5 inches?

8. A £2 coin has a diameter of 2.84 centimetres. How long is a straight line of 200 £2 coins when laid side by side? Give your answer in metres.

9. A pound coin is 3.15 millimetres thick. What is the height of a pile of 90 pound coins? Give your answer in centimetres.

10. Tap washers cost £0.06 each. What is the cost of 5000 of these washers?

11. 1 cm³ of platinum has a mass of 21.5 grams. Jane's platinum wedding ring has a volume of 0.5 cm³. What is the mass of the ring?

12. Turkish muslin is sold at £8.95 per metre. What is the cost of a 0.8 metre length?

13. French Camembert costs €13.45 per kilogram. How much does René pay for 0.3 kilogram of cheese? Give your answer to the nearest cent.

14. To turn marks into a percentage Mr Jackson multiplies them by 0.4 Hilary gets 141.5 marks. What is her percentage? Give your answer to the nearest whole number.

15. A marathon is 42.195 kilometres long. Unfortunately Mustapha has to retire after completing 0.6 of the course. How far has Mustapha run?

End of chapter activity: Chequered tiles (1)

Square black and white patterned tiles are placed in a line.

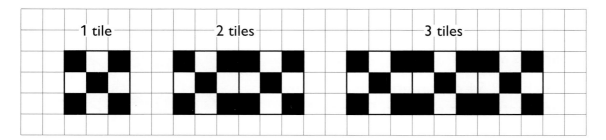

1. Draw a line of 4 tiles.

2. Copy and complete the table

Number of tiles	Number of black squares	Number of white squares	Total number of squares
1			
2			
3			
4			
5			

3. Answer these questions about the pattern.
   (a) How many black squares are there in a line of 20 tiles?
   (b) How many white squares are there in a line of 24 tiles?
   (c) What is the total number of squares in a line of 30 tiles?
   (d) How many tiles have a total of 225 black squares?
   (e) How many tiles have a total of 160 white squares?
   (f) How many tiles have a total of 234 squares altogether?
   (g) If there are 900 squares altogether how many of them are white?

Did you know?

Look at the pattern we can make with 1s.

1   × 1   = 1

11   × 11   = 121

111   × 111   = 12321

1111 × 1111 = 1234321

11111 × 11111 = 123454321

Chapter 13: Decimal division

We have already divided decimals when working out answers to problems involving money. Here is a reminder of how it works.

Examples:

$6.15 \div 5$ is the same as £6.15 ÷ 5

	1	.	2	3
5	6	.	¹1	¹5

(**Step 1:** $6 \div 5 = 1$, with 1 remainder. Write 1 in the answer line and carry 1)

(**Step 2:** $11 \div 5 = 2$, remainder 1)

(**Step 3:** $15 \div 5 = 3$)

Remember to put a decimal point in the answer line above the one in the question.

$6.15 \div 5 = 1.23$

(ii) $10.32 \div 4$ is the same as £10.32 ÷ 4

		2	.	5	8
4	1	0	.	²3	³2

(**Step 1:** $1 \div 4$ doesn't work, so look at $10 \div 4 = 2$, with 2 remainder. Write 2 in the answer line and carry 2)

(**Step 2:** $23 \div 4 = 5$, remainder 3)

(**Step 3:** $32 \div 4 = 8$)

$10.32 \div 4 = 2.58$

(iii) $2.16 \div 3$ is the same as £2.16 ÷ 3

	0	.	7	2
3	2	.	1	6

(**Step 1:** $2 \div 3$ doesn't work, so look at $21 \div 3 = 7$)

(**Step 2:** $6 \div 3 = 2$)

$2.16 \div 3 = 0.72$

Exercise 13.1: Dividing by a single integer

Calculate:

1. 5.8 ÷ 2
2. 8.7 ÷ 3
3. 9.2 ÷ 4
4. 8.5 ÷ 5
5. 7.8 ÷ 6

6. 5.6 ÷ 7
7. 7.2 ÷ 8
8. 6.3 ÷ 9
9. 33.2 ÷ 4
10. 48.5 ÷ 5

11. 75.6 ÷ 9
12. 60.2 ÷ 7
13. 51.6 ÷ 6
14. 28.8 ÷ 3
15. 37.6 ÷ 8

16. 29.2 ÷ 4
17. 17.2 ÷ 2
18. 8.35 ÷ 5
19. 6.72 ÷ 4
20. 1.96 ÷ 7

21. 9.52 ÷ 8
22. 0.85 ÷ 5
23. 0.14 ÷ 7
24. 88.5 ÷ 3
25. 94.2 ÷ 6

26. 53.6 ÷ 2
27. 88.2 ÷ 7
28. 79.5 ÷ 5
29. 97.6 ÷ 4
30. 82.4 ÷ 8

Decimal division with a remainder

Some division calculations do not produce an exact answer. When there is something left over, we call this a **remainder**.

Examples:

Divide 5.3 by 2

	2	• 6	
2	5	• ¹3	

(**Step 1:** 5 ÷ 2 = 2, with 1 remainder. Carry 1)
(**Step 2:** 13 ÷ 2 = 6 remainder 1)

However, we can continue to divide because we can add a 0 to the end of 5.3

Remember: 5.3 is the same as 5.30

	2	• 6	5
2	5	• ¹3	¹0

(**Step 3:** 10 ÷ 2 = 5)

5.3 ÷ 2 = 2.65

(ii)   Divide 6.5 by 4

	1	• 6	2	5
4	6	• ²5	¹0	²0

(**Step 1:** 6 ÷ 4 = 1, with 2 remainder. Carry 2)
(**Step 2:** 25 ÷ 4 = 6 remainder 1)
(**Step 3:** Add a zero, then 10 ÷ 4 = 2, with 2 remainder)
(**Step 4:** Add another zero, then 20 ÷ 4 = 5)

6.5 ÷ 4 = 1.625

You can also **add extra 0s** to the end of a number when you divide whole numbers. For example, 7.0 is the same as 7 and 4.00 is the same as 4

Put in as many 0s as you need, in order to complete the division.

Examples:

(i)   Calculate 9 ÷ 2

	4	• 5	
2	9	• ¹0	

(You need to add one extra 0)

9 ÷ 2 = 4.5

(ii) Calculate 13 ÷ 4

		3	· 2	5
4	1	3 · ¹0	²0	

(You need to add two extra 0s)

13 ÷ 4 = 3.25

(iii) Calculate 67 ÷ 8

		8	· 3	7	5
8	6	7 · ³0	⁶0	⁴0	

(You need to add three extra 0s)

67 ÷ 8 = 8.375

Exercise 13.2: Decimal division with a remainder

Calculate:

1. 5.3 ÷ 2
2. 1.8 ÷ 4
3. 7.6 ÷ 5
4. 8.7 ÷ 6
5. 17.2 ÷ 8

6. 3.8 ÷ 8
7. 14.7 ÷ 2
8. 33.1 ÷ 4
9. 23.9 ÷ 5
10. 19.5 ÷ 6

11. 1.98 ÷ 4
12. 7.12 ÷ 5
13. 6.3 ÷ 6
14. 1.85 ÷ 2
15. 0.12 ÷ 8

16. 5 ÷ 2
17. 14 ÷ 4
18. 17 ÷ 5
19. 3 ÷ 8
20. 47 ÷ 4

21. 27 ÷ 6

22. 72 ÷ 5

23. 20 ÷ 8

24. 65 ÷ 4

25. 31 ÷ 8

Dividing by multiples of 10, 100 and 1000

When we divide decimals by 10, 100 and 1000 we follow exactly the same rules as we do when we are working with whole numbers:

When we **divide by 10**, the digits move **1 place to the right**.

Th	H	T	U•	t	h	th
	2	7	3•			
		2	7•	3		

(273 ÷ 10)

When we **divide by 100**, the digits move **2 places to the right**.

Th	H	T	U•	t	h	th
	2	7	3•			
			2•	7	3	

(273 ÷ 100)

When we **divide by 1000**, the digits move **3 places to the right**.

Th	H	T	U•	t	h	th
	2	7	3•			
			0•	2	7	3

(273 ÷ 1000)

Examples:

(i)   Calculate 180 ÷ 20

We can think of 20 as 10 × 2

180 ÷ 10 = 18   (**Step 1:** Divide the decimal by the 10 first)

18 ÷ 2 = 9   (**Step 2:** Then divide by 2)

180 ÷ 20 = 9

(ii) Calculate 4200 ÷ 600

We can think of 600 as 100 × 6

4200 ÷ 100 = 42

42 ÷ 6 = 7

4200 ÷ 600 = 7

(You may find it useful to set out the following divisions in the formal way.)

		7
6	4	2

(iii) Calculate 75 000 ÷ 5000

We can think of 5000 as 1000 × 5

75 000 ÷ 1000 = 75

75 ÷ 5 = 15

75 000 ÷ 5000 = 15

	1	5
5	7	5

(iv) Calculate 625 ÷ 50

We can think of 50 as 10 × 5

625 ÷ 10 = 62.5

62.5 ÷ 5 = 12.5

625 ÷ 50 = 12.5

	1	2 • 5
5	6	¹2 •²5

(v) Calculate $3840 \div 400$

We can think of 400 as 100×4

$3840 \div 100 = 38.4$

$38.4 \div 4 = 9.6$

$3840 \div 400 = 9.6$

		9	•	6
4	3	8	•	²4

(vi) Calculate $4960 \div 8000$

We can think of 8000 as 1000×8

$4960 \div 1000 = 4.96(0)$

$4.96 \div 8 = 0.62$

$4960 \div 8000 = 0.62$

	0	•	6	2
8	4	•	9	¹6

Exercise 13.3: Dividing by multiples of 10, 100 and 1000

Calculate:

1. $160 \div 20$

2. $2700 \div 30$

3. $3500 \div 500$

4. $6400 \div 800$

5. $21\ 000 \div 7000$

6. $24\ 000 \div 4000$

7. $7200 \div 300$

8. $80\ 000 \div 5000$

9. $1760 \div 40$

10. $100\ 000 \div 200$

11. $576 \div 80$

12. $2940 \div 700$

13. $38\ 400 \div 6000$

14. $1350 \div 300$

15. $435 \div 50$

16. $1140 \div 2000$

17. $960 \div 400$

18. $9000 \div 60$

19. $42\ 000 \div 700$

20. $670\ 000 \div 5000$

Dividing by a decimal

So far you have always divided decimals by an integer (whole number).

We will now see what happens when you divide by a decimal.

The first thing to do when dividing by a decimal is to make the decimal a whole number. It makes the calculation a lot easier.

To make the decimal a whole number you must multiply it until the decimal disappears. You must also multiply the number being divided by the same amount. If you do this, the calculation remains the same. Here are some whole-number examples which show this.

Example:

$12 \div 4 = 3$ is the same as:

$24 \div 8 = 3$ (both 12 and 4 have been doubled and the answer is still 3)

$60 \div 20 = 3$ (both 12 and 4 have been multiplied by 5 and the answer is still 3)

$6 \div 2 = 3$ (both 12 and 4 have been halved and the answer is still 3)

When we want to make a decimal into a whole number, we multiply by a power of 10

Example:

$1.2 \div 0.4 = 3$ is the same as

$12 \div 4 = 3$ (both 1.2 and 0.4 have been multiplied by 10 and the answer is still 3)

Remember: Always divide by a whole number.

Examples:

(i) Calculate 5.6 ÷ 0.2

		2	8
2	5	¹6	

Step 1: Change 0.2 into a whole number (2) by multiplying it by 10

Step 2: 0.2 has been multiplied by 10, so we must also multiply 5.6 by 10, giving 56

Step 3: Now we can divide 56 by 2

(ii) Calculate 6.32 ÷ 0.4

	1	5 · 8
4	6 ²3 · ³2	

Step 1: 0.4 become 4 (× 10)

Step 2: 6.32 becomes 63.2 (× 10)

Step 3: Divide 63.2 by 4

6.32 ÷ 0.4 = 15.8

(iii) Calculate 0.738 ÷ 0.06

	1	2 · 3
6	7 ¹3 · ¹8	

Step 1: 0.06 become 6 (× 100)

Step 2: 0.738 becomes 73.8 (× 100)

Step 3: Divide 73.8 by 6

0.738 ÷ 0.06 = 12.3

(iv) Calculate 0.004 35 ÷ 0.005

	0 · 8	7
5	4 · 3	³5

Step 1: 0.005 become 5 (× 1000)

Step 2: 0.004 35 becomes 4.35 (× 1000)

Step 3: Divide 4.35 by 5

0.004 35 ÷ 0.005 = 0.87

(v) Calculate 17.6 ÷ 0.05

		3	5	2
5	1	7	²6	¹0

Step 1: 0.05 become 5 (× 100)

Step 2: 17.6 becomes 1760 (× 100 Notice that we have to add an extra **0** here.)

Step 3: Divide 1760 by 5

17.6 ÷ 0.05 = 352

Exercise 13.4: Dividing by a decimal

Calculate:

1. 4.6 ÷ 0.2
2. 8.5 ÷ 0.5
3. 7.8 ÷ 0.6
4. 0.57 ÷ 0.03
5. 0.45 ÷ 0.05

6. 0.068 ÷ 0.004
7. 5.85 ÷ 0.03
8. 3.85 ÷ 0.5
9. 0.315 ÷ 0.07
10. 0.344 ÷ 0.08

11. 0.001 52 ÷ 0.004
12. 7.894 ÷ 0.2
13. 1.251 ÷ 0.03
14. 23.64 ÷ 0.4
15. 2.418 ÷ 0.06

16. 0.1575 ÷ 0.05
17. 21.21 ÷ 0.7
18. 0.009 52 ÷ 0.008
19. 0.135 ÷ 0.3
20. 0.0456 ÷ 0.6

21. 0.57 ÷ 0.2
22. 0.135 ÷ 0.06
23. 4.386 ÷ 0.05
24. 2.63 ÷ 0.4
25. 0.18 ÷ 0.8

26. 43 ÷ 0.2
27. 21.6 ÷ 0.04
28. 0.49 ÷ 0.002
29. 84 ÷ 0.8
30. 1.67 ÷ 0.005

End of chapter activity: Chequered tiles (2)

Alternate squares are black or white as shown in these patterns.

Pattern 1   Pattern 2   Pattern 3

1. Draw pattern 4

2. Copy and complete the table.

Pattern number	Number of black squares	Number of white squares	Total number of squares
1	1	0	1
2			
3			
4			
5			81

3. Answer these questions about the pattern:

   (a) Pattern 12 has 265 black squares.

   How many white squares are there in pattern 12?

   (b) Pattern 13 has 312 white squares.

   How many black squares are there in pattern 13?

   (c) Pattern 15 has a total of 841 squares.

   How many of these squares are black?

Did you know?

In 1202 Leonardo of Pisa, better known as Fibonacci, produced a sequence of numbers which have been named after him:

- the first number is 0
- the second number is 1
- each subsequent number is equal to the sum of the two previous numbers of the sequence.

0	1	1	2	3	5	8
		(1 + 0)	(1 + 1)	(2 + 1)	(3 + 2)	(5 + 3)

See if you can continue the sequence – a calculator will help (the 20th number in the sequence is 4181).

The Fibonacci number is seen in nature. For example, the number of petals on a flower is often one of the Fibonacci numbers.

Chapter 14: Long multiplication

When you multiply by more than one digit the multiplication calculation is called **long multiplication**.

Multiplying using factors

Sometime it is easier to break a multiplication down into steps, using factors.

Multiplying by 8, for example, is the same as multiplying by 4 and then by 2

This is because 2 and 4 are the factors of 8:

$$25 \times 8 = 200$$

This calculation can be broken down into 2 parts and will still give us the same answer:

Step 1: $25 \times 4 = 100$

Step 2: $100 \times 2 = 200$

This method can be very helpful when multiplying by more than one digit.

Examples:

(i) Multiply 57 by 15

The factors of 15 are 5×3

Step 1: Multiply by 5

	H	T	U	
		5	7	$(7 \times 5 = 35)$
×			5	$(5 \times 5 = 25$ plus carried 3)
	2	8	5	
		₃		

Step 2: Multiply by 3

H	T	U
	2	8	5
×			3
	8	5	5
	2	1	

(5 × 3 = 15)

(8 × 3 = 24 plus carried 1)

(2 × 3 = 6 plus carried 2)

57 × 15 = 855

(ii) Multiply 476 by 28

The factors of 28 are 7 × 4

Step 1: Multiply by 7

Th	H	T	U
	4	7	6
×			7
3	3	3	2
	5	4	

(6 × 7 = 42)

(7 × 7 = 49 plus carried 4)

(4 × 7 = 28 plus carried 5)

Step 2: Multiply by 4

	Th	H	T	U
	3	3	3	2
×				4
1	3	3	2	8
	1	1		

(2 × 4 = 8)

(3 × 4 = 12)

(3 × 4 = 12 plus carried 1)

(3 × 4 = 12 plus carried 1)

476 × 28 = 13 328

Exercise 14.1: Multiplying using factors

Calculate, using factors:

1. 31 × 15
2. 57 × 28
3. 93 × 12
4. 47 × 24
5. 71 × 18

6. 67 × 32
7. 29 × 25
8. 83 × 14
9. 25 × 35
10. 51 × 16

11. 63 × 48
12. 73 × 54
13. 23 × 72
14. 85 × 63
15. 19 × 49

16. 46 × 56
17. 28 × 42
18. 53 × 36
19. 17 × 64
20. 37 × 45

21. 417 × 12
22. 539 × 35
23. 346 × 42
24. 189 × 27
25. 817 × 18

26. 231 × 56
27. 782 × 32
28. 853 × 63
29. 604 × 24
30. 138 × 72

Informal multiplication by partition

Here are a couple of informal ways of doing long multiplication.

Examples:

(i) Multiply 64 by 37

Method 1:

$64 \times 37 = 64 \times (30 + 7)$ (Partition (split) 37 into **Tens** and **Units**.)

Step 1: First calculate 64×30

$$64 \times 30 = 64 \times 10 \times 3$$
$$= 640 \times 3 \qquad (64 \times 10 = 640)$$
$$= 1920$$

Step 2: Now calculate 64×7

	H	T	U
		6	4
×			7
	4	4	8
		2	

Step 3: Add the answers to Step 1 and Step 2 together:

	Th	H	T	U
		1	9	2	0
+			4	4	8
		2	3	6	8
		1			

$64 \times 37 = 2368$

Method 2: Another informal method is to partition (split) both the numbers using a grid like this:

×	60	4	
30	1800	120	= 1920
7	420	28	= 448
			= 2368

(ii) Multiply 473 by 29

Method 1:

$473 \times 29 = 473 \times (20 + 9)$

Step 1: First calculate 473×20

$$473 \times 20 = 473 \times 10 \times 2$$
$$= 4730 \times 2$$
$$= 9460$$

Step 2: Now calculate 473×9

	Th	H	T	U
		4	7	3
×				9
	4	2	5	7
		6	2	

Step 3: Add the answers to Step 1 and Step 2 together:

		Th	H	T	U
		9	4	6	0
+		4	2	5	7
	1	3	7	1	7
			1		

$473 \times 29 = 13\ 717$

Method 2:

×	400	70	3	
20	8000	1400	60	= 9460
9	3600	630	27	= 4257
				= 13 717

Exercise 14.2: Informal multiplication by partition

Calculate, using an informal method:

1. 93 × 13
2. 47 × 19
3. 37 × 23
4. 91 × 27
5. 69 × 39

6. 48 × 54
7. 18 × 57
8. 49 × 17
9. 36 × 29
10. 87 × 65

11. 415 × 23
12. 643 × 34
13. 132 × 17
14. 218 × 92
15. 426 × 73

16. 563 × 47
17. 271 × 53
18. 737 × 63
19. 817 × 71
20. 903 × 87

Multiplying using the formal method

These examples show the informal method above written in a formal way.

Examples:

(i)   Multiply 64 by 37

Th	H	T	U
		6	4
×		3	7
	4	4	8
1	9	2	0
2	3	6	8

(Multiply 64 by 7)

(Multiply 64 by 30 This will end in 0)

(Add the two results.)

(ii) Multiply 473 by 29

Th	H	T	U
	4	7	3
×		2	9
	4	2	5	7
	9	4	6	0
1	3	7	1	7

(Multiply 473 by 9)

(Multiply 473 by 20 This will end in 0)

(Add the two results.)

Exercise 14.3: Multiplying using the formal method

Calculate the following, using the formal method:

1.   47 × 23

2.   72 × 51

3.   67 × 83

4.   95 × 34

5.   26 × 47

6.   39 × 75

7.   52 × 92

8.   82 × 63

9.   59 × 37

10. 17 × 89

11. 253 × 17

12. 729 × 41

13. 347 × 78

14. 806 × 23

15. 632 × 37

16. 519 × 84

17. 183 × 97

18. 485 × 57

19. 650 × 63

20. 701 × 29

Exercise 14.4: Problem solving

1. A bus can carry 86 passengers when full. What is the most number of people that 15 buses can carry?

2. A carton contains 48 packets of butter. How many packets are there in 36 cartons?

3. 50 years ago grandfather's car travelled 37 miles on 1 gallon of petrol. How many miles could he cover on 16 gallons?

4. February has 28 days. How many hours are there in February?

5. A sheet of sticky labels consists of 32 rows each containing 42 labels. How many labels are there in a sheet?

6. There are 26 rows of seats at the Grand Theatre. Each row has 38 seats in it. How many seats are there in the theatre?

7. An ICT expert is paid £435 per day. How much does she earn in 21 days?

8. Ozzie is paid to shear 260 sheep in a day. How many sheep does he shear in 25 days?

9. A bicycle shop takes delivery of 18 cycles which cost £329 each. How much does it cost the owner to buy these cycles?

10. 72 people each pay £963 for a cruise. How much do they pay altogether?

End of chapter activity: Squares and crosses

Squares with sides measuring 1 unit make a pattern of crosses:

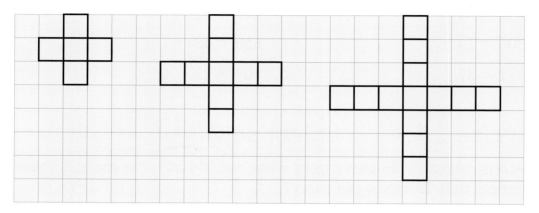

1. Draw pattern 4 in the sequence above.

2. Copy and complete the table:

Length of arms (units)	Area of cross (units²)	Length of perimeter (units)
1	5	12
2	9	20
3	13	28
4		
5		

3. Answer these questions about the pattern:
   (a) What is the area of a cross with arms 9 units long?
   (b) What is the perimeter of a cross with arms 10 units long?
   (c) What is the connection between the area and the length of the perimeter?
   (d) A cross has an area of 101 units².

   What is the perimeter of this cross?

Did you know?

Multiply 37 037 by any single number (1–9), then multiply that number by 3. Every digit in the answer will be the same as that first single number. Try it with your calculator.

Chapter 15: Division using factors

In Chapter 14 we looked at multiplication by factors. Now we are going to look at division by factors.

Miss Plunkett wants to divide a box of 288 strawberries among the 16 children in her class.

She knows the calculation $288 \div 16$ will give the answer to how many strawberries each child will receive. Unfortunately Miss Plunkett does not know her 16 times table! What can she do? She does know her 2 to 10 times tables.

Miss Plunkett decides to divide the children into 2 groups and give each group half the strawberries. Now there are 2 groups of 8 children, each with 144 strawberries. Each child will receive $144 \div 8 = 18$ strawberries.

How would Miss Plunkett write down the calculations she has performed?

		1	4	4
2	2	8	8	

and

			1	8
8	1	4	⁶4	

Miss Plunkett has divided by the factors of 16 ($2 \times 8 = 16$).

Example:

Divide 819 by 21

The factors of 21 are 3×7

Step 1: Divide by 3

		2	7	3
3	8	²1	9	

Step 2: Divide by 7

			3	9
7	2	7	⁶3	

$819 \div 21 = 39$

It does not matter in which order you divide.

Example:

Divide 7904 by 32

The factors of 32 are 4 × 8

Step 1: Divide by 4

		1	9	7	6
4	7	^{3}9	^{3}0	^{2}4	

Step 2: Divide by 8

			2	4	7
8	1	9	^{3}7	^{5}6	

or: **Step 1:** Divide by 8

			9	8	8
8	7	9	^{7}0	^{6}4	

Step 2: Divide by 4

		2	4	7
4	9	^{1}8	^{2}8	

Exercise 15.1: Division using factors

Calculate the following using factors. All the answers are exact – there are no remainders.

1. 270 ÷ 18
2. 864 ÷ 24
3. 780 ÷ 15
4. 532 ÷ 28
5. 912 ÷ 16

6. 602 ÷ 14
7. 928 ÷ 32
8. 987 ÷ 21
9. 828 ÷ 36
10. 798 ÷ 42

11. 1140 ÷ 15
12. 1024 ÷ 16
13. 1806 ÷ 21
14. 1536 ÷ 24
15. 1863 ÷ 27

16. 2716 ÷ 28
17. 1665 ÷ 45
18. 2296 ÷ 56
19. 2142 ÷ 63
20. 4214 ÷ 49

21. 7749 ÷ 63
22. 4000 ÷ 32
23. 4464 ÷ 24
24. 7560 ÷ 35
25. 9548 ÷ 28

26. 10 374 ÷ 21
27. 25 788 ÷ 42
28. 15 552 ÷ 48
29. 31 416 ÷ 56
30. 39 024 ÷ 72

Exercise 15.2: Problem solving

1. 35 children divide 280 apples equally between them. How many apples does each child receive?

2. In a car park there is room for 630 cars in 15 equal lines. How many parking spaces are there in a line?

3. 414 chairs are laid out in the Church Hall in 18 equal rows. How many chairs are there in a row?

4. 768 recruits are divided into 24 squads. How many recruits are there in a squad?

5. Geoff uses 48 litres of petrol to travel 1104 kilometres on his motorcycle. How far does he go on 1 litre of petrol?

6. Eggs are placed on trays that hold 64 eggs. How many trays are needed to hold 1088 eggs?

7. 27 teachers share a Lotto win of £6966 equally. What is each teacher's share?

8. 1728 box files, which are all the same size, are arranged on 32 shelves of the same length. How many box files are there on a shelf?

9. Norman buys 16 packets of tulip bulbs. How many bulbs are there in a packet if the total number of bulbs is 1200?

10. 56 tubes of Witties contain 2128 chocolate drops. How many drops are there in a tube?

End of chapter activity: Dots and lines

Squares made up of 4 lines and 4 dots are drawn in the following pattern

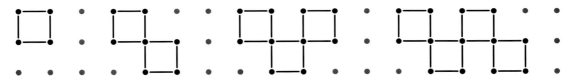

1. Draw the pattern with five squares.

2. Copy and complete the table.

Number of squares	Number of lines	Number of dots
1	4	4
2		7
3	12	
4		
5		

3. Answer these questions about the patterns.
   (a) How many lines are there in the pattern of 20 squares?
   (b) How many dots are there in the pattern of 30 squares?
   (c) How many squares are there in the pattern that has 200 lines?
   (d) How many squares are there in the pattern with 301 dots?

Did you know?

Look at this interesting number pattern using consecutive numbers.

$$1 + 2 = 3 \tag{3}$$

$$4 + 5 + 6 = 7 + 8 \tag{15}$$

$$9 + 10 + 11 + 12 = 13 + 14 + 15 \tag{42}$$

$$16 + 17 + 18 + 19 + 20 = 21 + 22 + 23 + 24 \tag{90}$$

$$25 + 26 + 27 + 28 + 29 + 30 = 31 + 32 + 33 + 34 + 35 \tag{165}$$

What comes next?

Chapter 16: Angles

An **angle** is formed at the point at which two lines meet.

One line   Two lines

Measuring angles

We can measure the size of an angle by using a protractor.

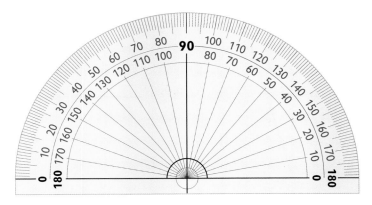

The angle being measured here is 50°.

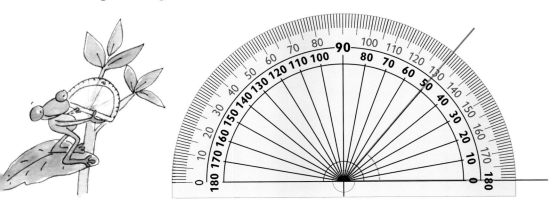

When measuring angles, remember:
- Make sure you know whether the answer will be more or less than 90°.
- Make sure you use the correct scale (inside or outside).

Exercise 16.1: Measuring angles

Measure and write down the size of each of these angles:

1.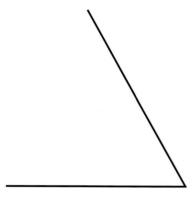

2.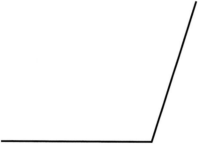

3.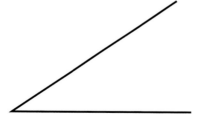

4.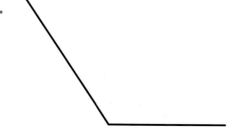

5.

6.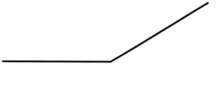

7.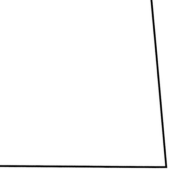

8.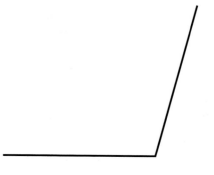

Hint: For Q9–12 you might find it helpful to turn the page so that one of the lines is horizontal in front of you, as in Q1–8

9.

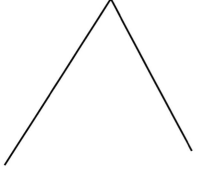

11.

10.

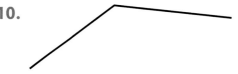

12.

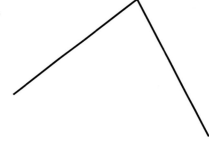

Drawing angles

When drawing angles, remember:

●   Estimate the size of the angle by rotating your pencil.

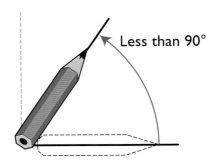

Less than 90°

More than 90°

●   Make sure you use the correct scale (inside or outside).

Exercise 16.2: Drawing angles

For each question, start by drawing a line about 6 centimetres long and letter it AB.

Draw the following angles:

1. angle A = 60°
2. angle B = 120°
3. angle A = 46°
4. angle A = 124°
5. angle B = 73°

6. angle B = 112°
7. angle A = 52°
8. angle B = 131°
9. angle B = 28°
10. angle A = 145°

11. angle B = 85°
12. angle A = 105°
13. angle B = 163°
14. angle A = 34°
15. angle A = 97°

16. angle B = 83°
17. angle B = 155°
18. angle B = 55°
19. angle A = 69°
20. angle A = 134°

Angles on a straight line

When a line is rotated through two right angles it has moved through 180° (90° × 2) and forms one longer straight line.

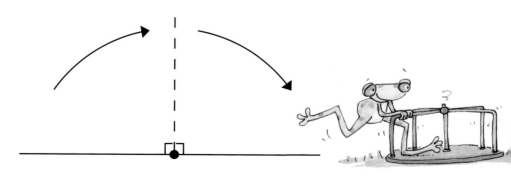

When another line is drawn to meet a straight line two angles are formed.

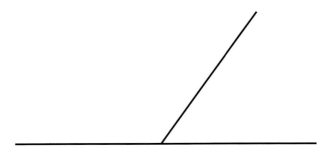

It follows that the two angles will add up to 180°.

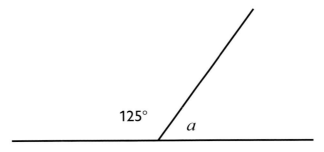

To find the size of angle a, subtract the given angle from **180°**.

angle a = **180° − 125°**

= **55°**

Exercise 16.3: Angles on a straight line

Calculate the size of the angles marked a.

1.

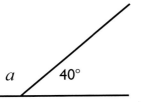

2.

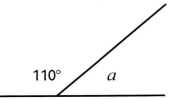

3.

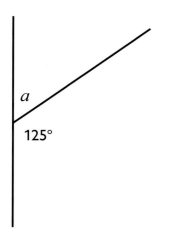

a

125°

7.

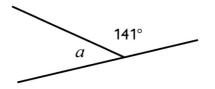

141°

a

8.

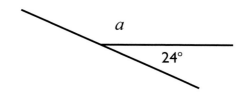

a

24°

4.

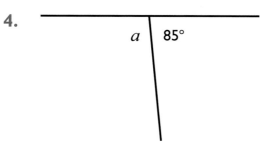

a   85°

9.

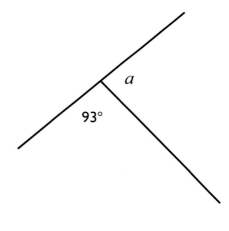

a

93°

5.

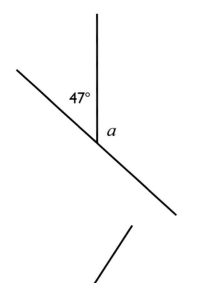

47°

a

10.

165°

a

6.

a

118°

Angles round a point

When a line is rotated through a whole revolution it has moved through 360° (4 right angles).

As for angles on a straight line, if we know one of the angles around a point, we can work out the other one.

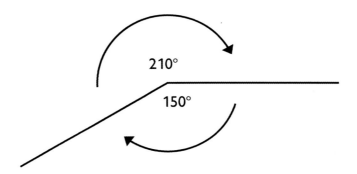

If one angle is 150° the other is 210° (360° − 150°).

Vertically opposite angles

In the diagram below, AB and CD are straight lines.

$a + b + c + d = 360°$ (angles round a point)

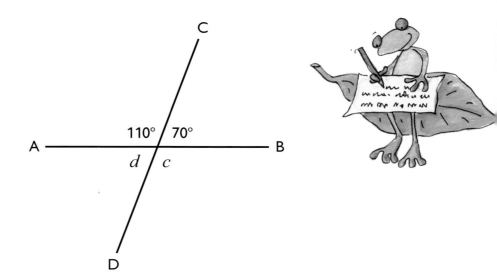

If $a = 110°$ then $b = 70°$ (angles on the straight line AB add up to 180°)

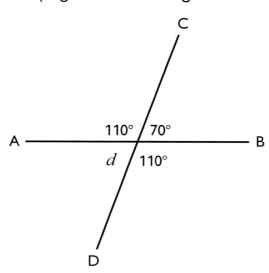

If $b = 70°$ then $c = 110°$ (angles on the straight line CD add up to 180°)

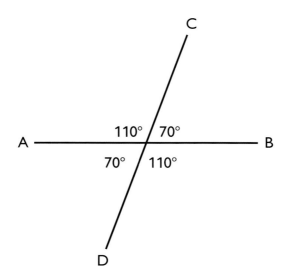

If $c = 110°$ then $d = 70°$ (angles on the straight line AB add up to 180°)

                    or   (angles on the straight line CD add up to 180°)

                    or   (angles round a point add up to 360°)

This shows us that when two straight lines intersect (cut each other), two pairs of equal angles are formed. The angles which are **vertically opposite** each other are equal.

Exercise 16.4: Angles

Calculate the size of the angles marked with the small letters. In each diagram, AB and CD are straight lines.

1.

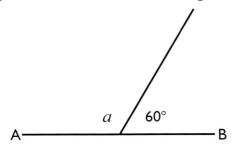

2.

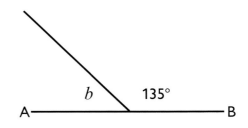

3.

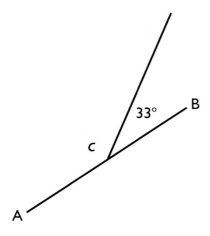

6.

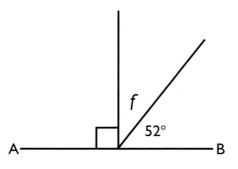

4.

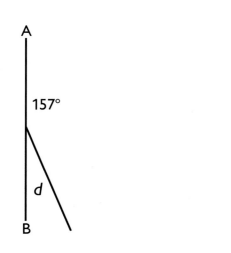

7.

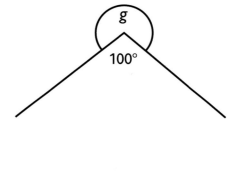

5.

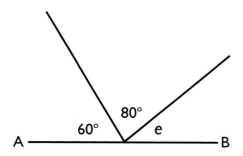

8.

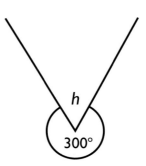

9.

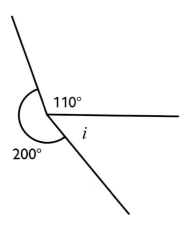

10.

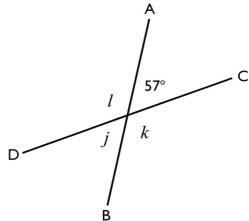

The sum of the angles in a triangle

We are going to learn about the sum of the angles of a triangle by working through the following exercise.

Exercise 16.5:
The sum of the angles in a triangle

1. Start by drawing any triangle and mark each of the angles with a different colour.

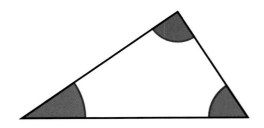

2. Now cut off the angles.

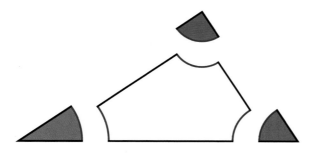

3. Next draw a straight line and mark a point on it.

4. Place the angles at the point on the line.

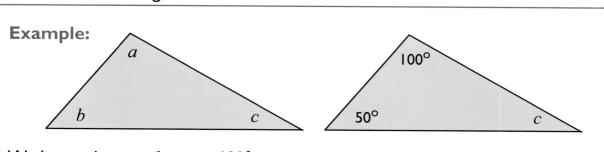

What do you notice?

The three angles from a triangle can be arranged in a straight line. This tells us that they add up to 180°.

Angles and triangles

You have learnt that the sum of the angles in a triangle is 180°. This means that, if you know the size of two of the angles in a triangle, you can find the size of the third angle.

Example:

We know that $a + b + c = 180°$

> If a = 100 and b = 50, then:
>
> $$100 + 50 + c = 180$$
> $$c = 180 - 100 - 50 \text{ or } 180 - (100 + 50)$$
> $$c = 30°$$

There are two special types of triangles.

Isosceles triangle

An **isosceles triangle** is symmetrical. It has:

● a pair of equal sides;
● a pair of equal angles (these are opposite the equal sides).

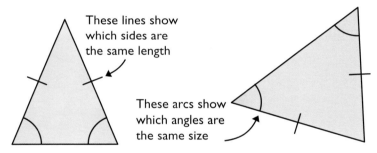

These lines show which sides are the same length

These arcs show which angles are the same size

If you know the size of one angle, you can find the size of the other two.

Hint: Always start by marking in the equal angles.

Examples:

(i) Calculate the size of angle a.

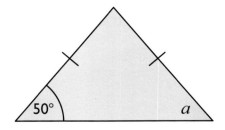

a = 50° (it is the other angle opposite the equal sides)

(ii) Calculate the size of angle b.

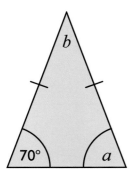

$a = 70°$ (the other equal angle)

$b = 180 - 140$ (sum of angles of triangle, $70 + 70 = 140$)

   $= 40°$

(iii) Calculate the size of angle c.

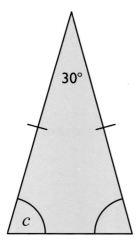

The 2 unknown angles $= 180 - 30$ (sum of angles of triangle)

                    $= 150°$

They are equal (angles opposite equal sides), so

                $c = 150 \div 2$

                  $= 75°$

Equilateral triangle

An equilateral triangle is a triangle where:

- all sides are equal;
- all angles are equal ($180 \div 3 = 60°$).

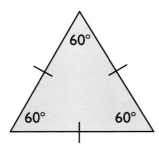

Exercise 16.6: Angles and triangles

Calculate the size of the angles marked with small letters:

1.

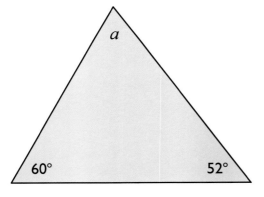

2.

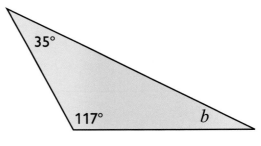

3.

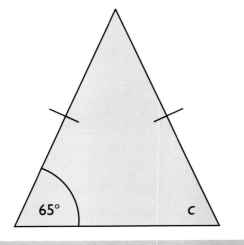

4.

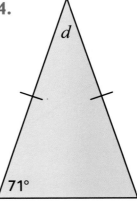

5.

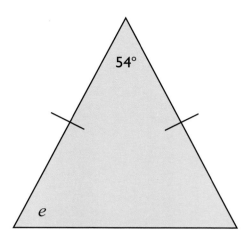

8.

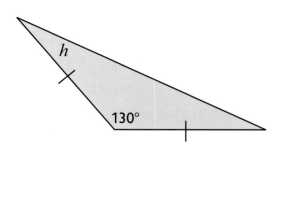

6.

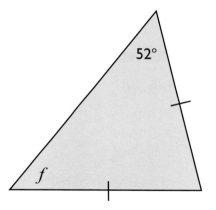

9.

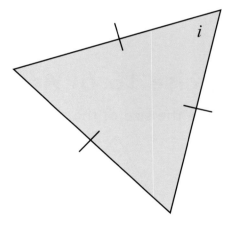

7.

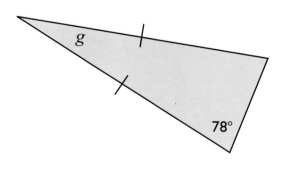

10.

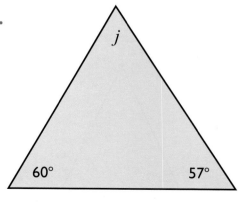

Summary

Make sure you understand and remember the following facts.

- Angles on a straight line add up to 180°.
- Angles round a point add up to 360°.
- Vertically opposite angles are equal.
- The sum of the angles in a triangle is 180°.
- An isosceles triangle has two equal sides and two equal angles.
- An equilateral triangle has three equal sides and three equal angles (60°).

Exercise 16.7: Summary exercise

Calculate the size of the angles marked with small letters:

1. AB is a straight line.

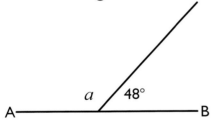

2. AB is a straight line.

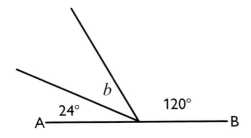

3.

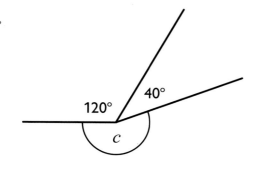

4. AB and CD are straight lines.

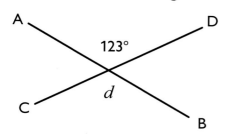

5.

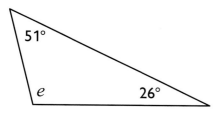

6.

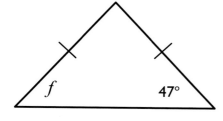

7.

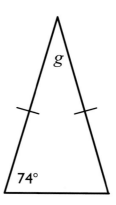

8.

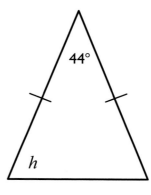

9.

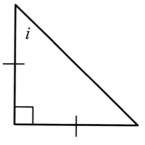

10.

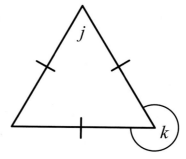

End of chapter activity: Equilateral triangles

Equilateral triangles form a pattern. Each triangle is drawn with three lines and has a dot at each vertex.

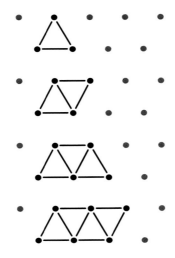

1. Draw the pattern with five triangles.

2. Copy and complete the table.

Number of triangles	Number of dots	Number of lines
1	3	3
2		5
3	5	
4		
5		

3. Answer these questions about the patterns.
   (a) How many dots are there in the pattern with 12 triangles?
   (b) If the pattern has 20 triangles, how many lines are there?
   (c) How many triangles are needed to produce a pattern with 73 dots?
   (d) How many triangles are there in the pattern made up of 121 lines?

Did you know?

Here is an interesting mathematical pattern.

$$(0 \times 9) + 1 = 1$$
$$(1 \times 9) + 2 = 11$$
$$(12 \times 9) + 3 = 111$$
$$(123 \times 9) + 4 = 1111$$
$$(1234 \times 9) + 5 = 11111$$

What are the next few calculations in the sequence? Is the pattern still true?

Chapter 17: Translation

Moving a point or shape in straight lines is called **translation**.

We always translate the point or shape in this order:

1. horizontally (right or left)
2. vertically (up or down)

Reading translations

We read translations by counting squares.

Examples:

(i)

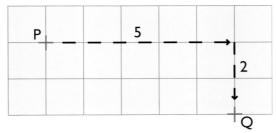

P has been translated 5 squares right then
2 squares down.

The new point, or **image**, is called Q.

(ii)

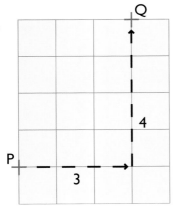

P has been translated 3 squares right then
4 squares up.

(iii)

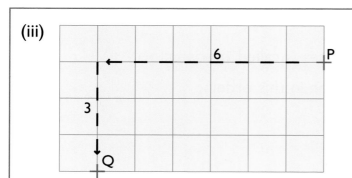

P has been translated 6 squares left then
3 squares down.

(iv)

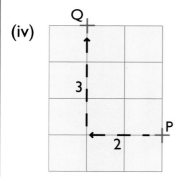

P has been translated 2 squares left then
3 squares up.

Exercise 17.1: Reading translations

Write down the translation that moves P to Q.

1.

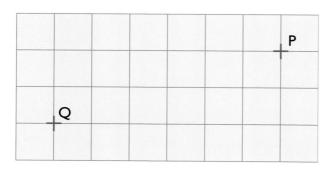

2.

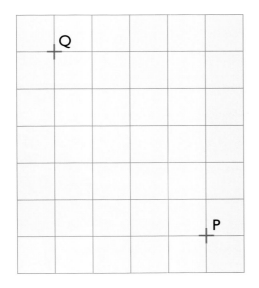

3.

4.

5.

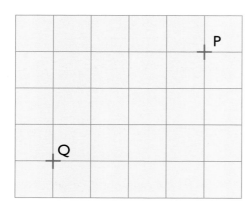

8.

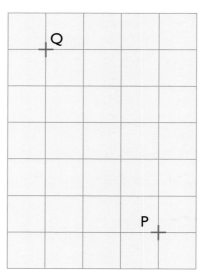

6.

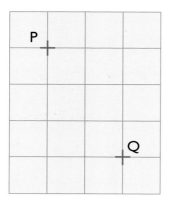

7.

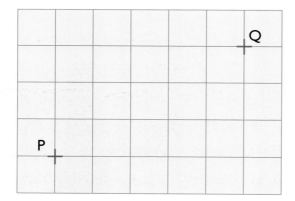

Plotting translations

To plot a translation, remember to count horizontally and then vertically.

Example:

> Translate P by 4 squares right followed by 3 squares down.
> Label the image Q.
> Count 4 squares horizontally to the right followed by 3 squares vertically down.

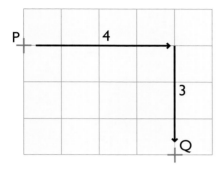

Exercise 17.2: Plotting translations

Mark the point P at the centre of a piece of squared paper.

Then plot the following translations of the point P.

1. 7 squares right followed by 2 squares up. Label the image A.
2. 2 squares left followed by 6 squares down. Label the image B.
3. 4 squares left followed by 6 squares up. Label the image C.
4. 4 squares right followed by 7 squares down. Label the image D.
5. 1 square left followed by 3 squares up. Label the image E.
6. 5 squares left followed by 3 squares down. Label the image F.
7. 3 squares right followed by 5 squares up. Label the image G.
8. 6 squares right followed by 2 squares down. Label the image H.
9. 6 squares left. Label the image I.
10. 5 squares down. Label the image J.

Using a grid

A grid can be used with translation. The rules are the same.

Movement horizontally right or left is movement **parallel to the x axis**.

Movement vertically up or down is movement **parallel to the y axis**.

We measure the **length of movement** in **units** (not squares). A unit is the distance between consecutive whole numbers on the axes.

Hint: Always decide what a unit is before answering the question. Look at the scales of the axes carefully.

Examples:

(i) Write down the translation that moves P to Q

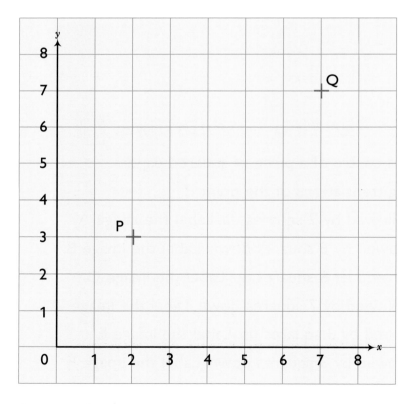

1 unit is 1 square.

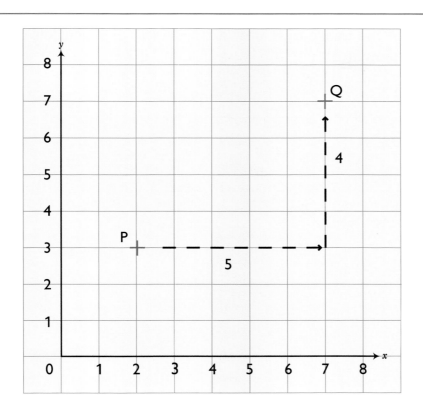

The translation is 5 units right followed by 4 units up.

(ii) Plot the position of the image of P after a translation of 1 unit left followed by 2 units down.

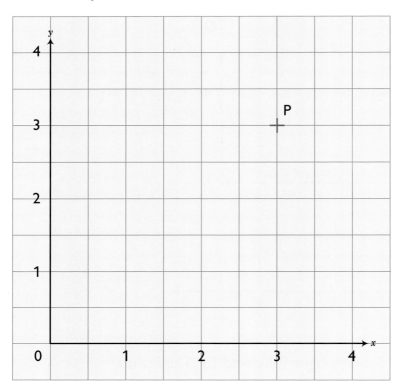

Label the image Q.

1 unit is 2 squares.

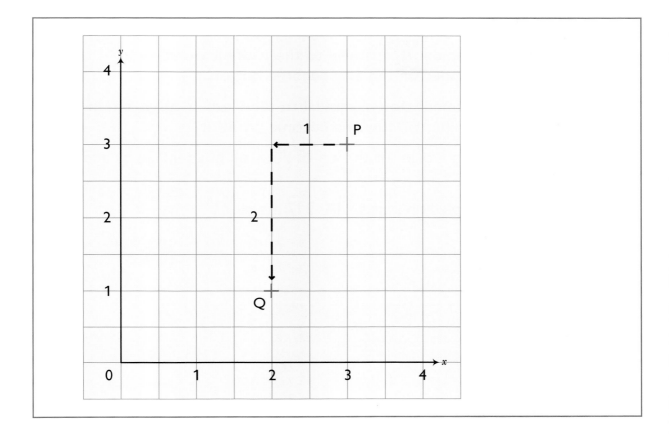

Positive and negative direction

We can use the words positive and negative to describe the **direction** of movement in a translation.

Think of a number line. Imagine that you are starting at 0

● If you move to the **right**, the numbers get **larger**, and they are **positive**.

● If you move to the **left**, the numbers get **smaller**, and they are **negative**.

Now imagine that the number line is the *x axis* of a grid.

● We say that movement to the **right**, parallel to the *x* axis, is **positive** in direction. The number on the axis becomes **larger**.

● We say that movement to the **left**, parallel to the *x* axis, is **negative** in direction. The number on the axis becomes **smaller**.

Now imagine that your number line is vertical, the **y axis** of a grid.

● We say that movement **up**, parallel to the *y* axis, is **positive** in direction. The number on the axis become **larger**.

● We say that movement **down**, parallel to the *y* axis, is **negative** in direction. The number on the axis become **smaller**.

This means that we can work out the **co-ordinates** of an image by adding or subtracting.

Let's look at the Examples on pages 214–217 again.

Examples:

(i) P starts at (2, 3)

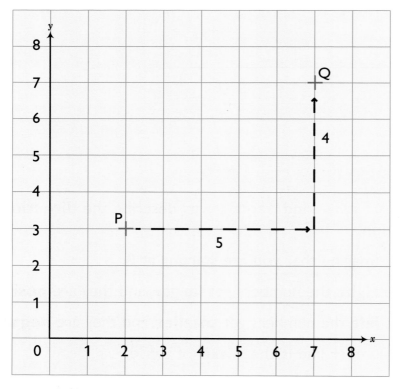

The translation is positive in both directions.

It adds 5 to the *x* co-ordinate $2 + 5 = 7$

It adds 4 to the *y* co-ordinate $3 + 4 = 7$

So the image Q is at (7, 7).

(ii)   P starts at (3, 3)

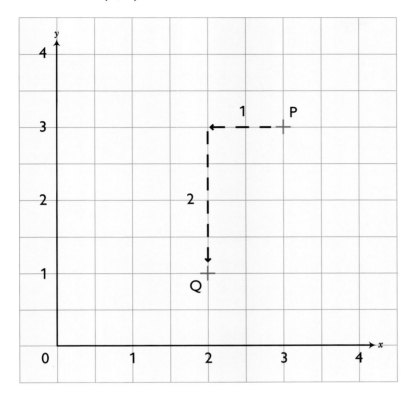

The translation is negative in both directions.

It subtracts 1 from the x co-ordinate   3 − 1 = 2

It subtracts 2 from the y co-ordinate   3 − 2 = 1

So the image Q is at (2, 1).

You can use this to check your answers.

Exercise 17.3: Using a grid

1. Write down the translation that moves P to:

    (a) A   (f) F
    (b) B   (g) G
    (c) C   (h) H
    (d) D   (i) I
    (e) E   (j) J

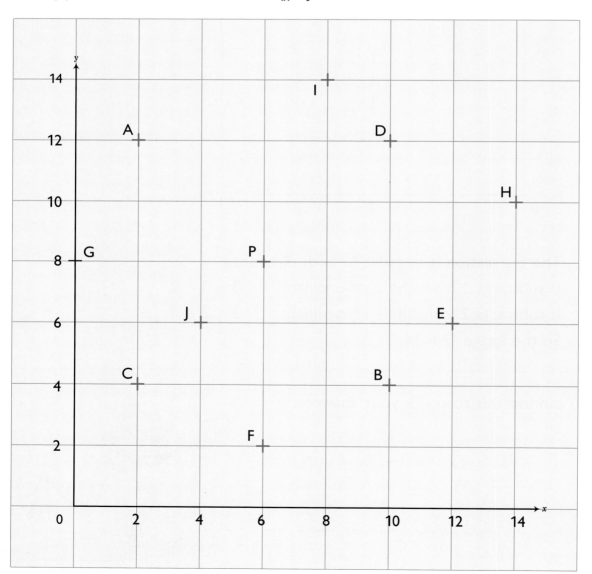

2. On a copy of the grid below, plot the following translations to the point P.

(a) 3 units left followed by 4 units up. Label the image A.

(b) 4 units right followed by 2 units up. Label the image B.

(c) 3 units right followed by 6 units down. Label the image C.

(d) 4 units left followed by 5 units down. Label the image D.

(e) +3 followed by +1   Label the image E.

(f) −2 followed by +3   Label the image F.

(g) +2 followed by −4   Label the image G.

(h) −1 followed by −3   Label the image H.

(i) −5 followed by 0   Label the image I.

(j) 0 followed by −6   Label the image J.

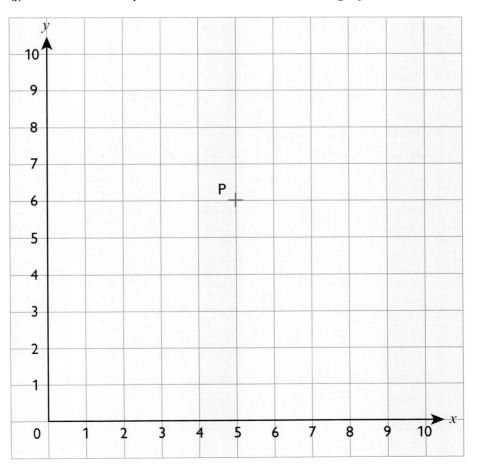

Translation of shapes

To translate a shape, move each **vertex** (corner) by the given translation.

Example:

Translate triangle ABC 7 squares right followed by 2 squares down.

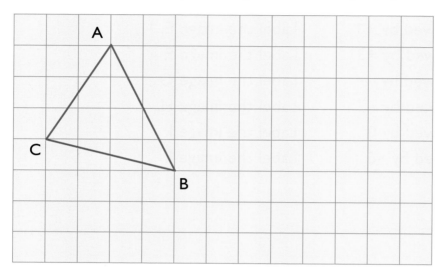

Label the image PQR. (Remember, the order of the letters stays the same. A becomes P, B becomes Q and C becomes R.)

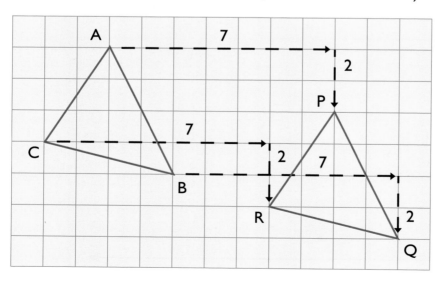

Notice that the shape stays the same way round. This is because each vertex moves the same distance. This means that you can count units for one vertex only, and then just copy the rest of the shape.

Example:

Translate ABCD 5 units left followed by 3 units down.

Label the image WXYZ.

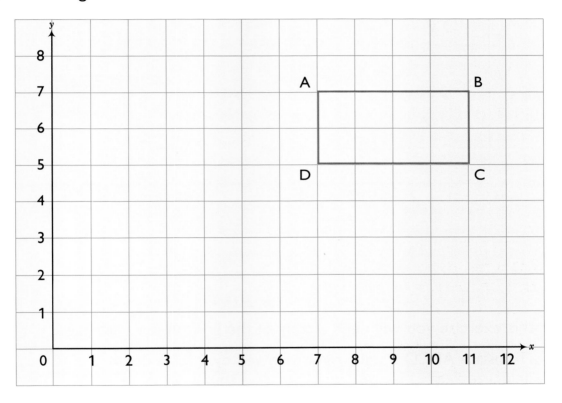

Translate the top left-hand corner.

Copy the rest of the rectangle.

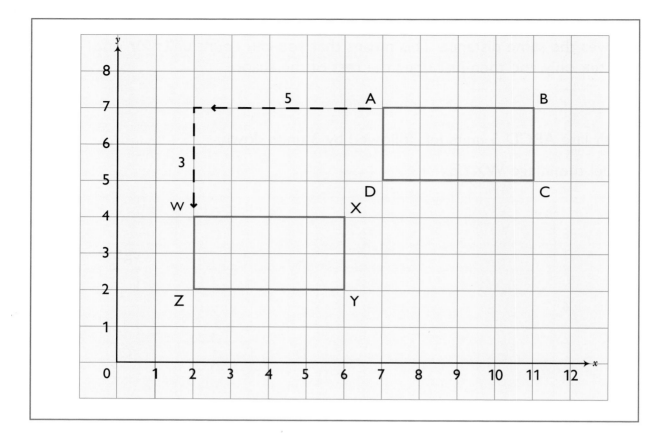

Exercise 17.4: Translation of shapes (1)

For this exercise you will need a copy of the grid on the next page.

1. Translate ABCD 5 units right followed by 4 units down.
   Label the image PQRS.

2. Translate DEF 6 units left followed by 4 units up.
   Label the image XYZ.

3. Translate LMN 6 units right followed by 10 units up.
   Label the image UVW.

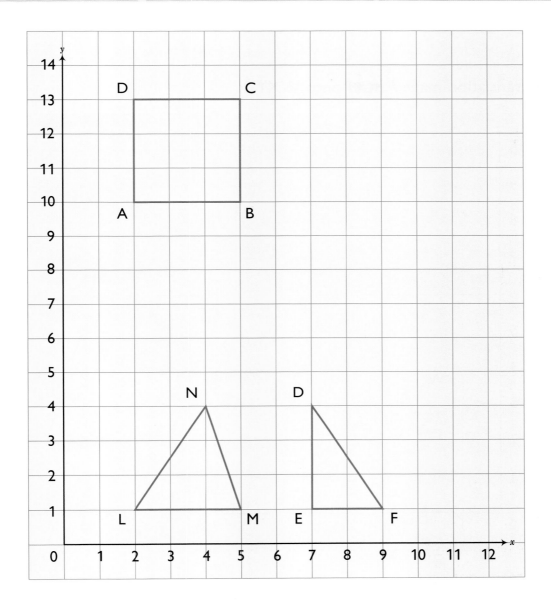

To read what translation has taken place:

- choose a vertex on the shape and identify the corresponding vertex on the image;

- work out the horizontal movement;

- work out the vertical movement.

Example:

What translation maps ABCD onto WXYZ?

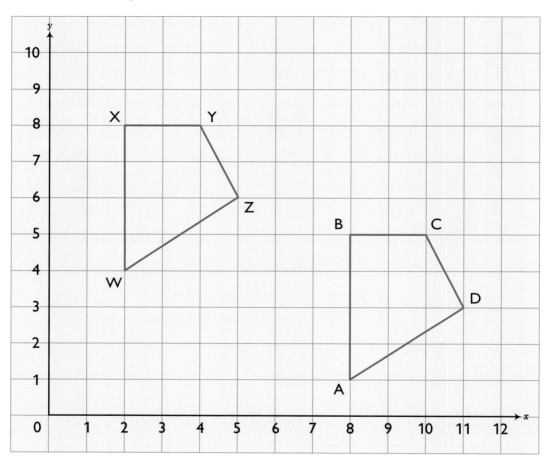

- A maps onto W.
- Horizontal movement is 6 units to the left.
- Vertical movement is 3 units up.

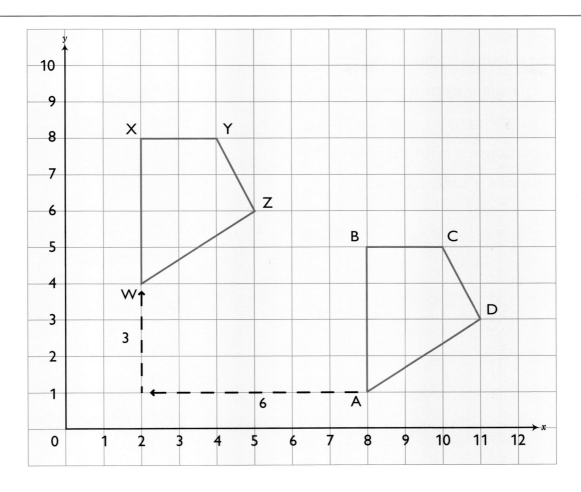

The translation is 6 units to the left followed by 3 units up.

Exercise 17.5: Translation of shapes (2)

Write down the translation that maps:

1.   triangle a onto triangle b;

2.   parallelogram c onto parallelogram d;

3.   rectangle e onto rectangle f;

4.   square g onto square h.

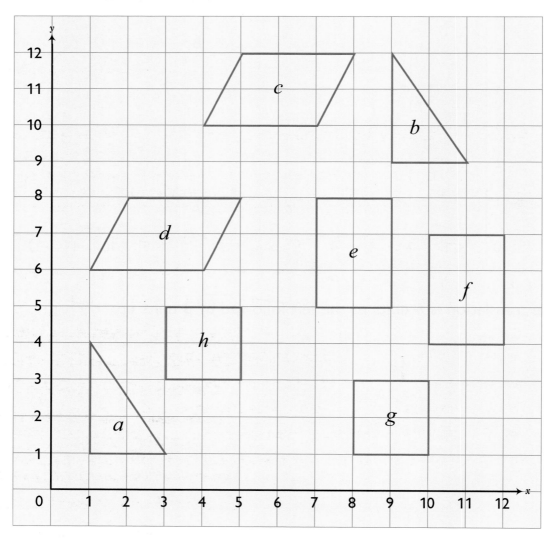

End of chapter activity: Lots of L-shapes

A pattern of L shapes is made up of 1 centimetre squares.

Pattern 1   Pattern 2   Pattern 3

1. Draw pattern 4

2. Copy and complete the table.

Pattern number	Number of squares	Length of perimeter (cm)
1	3	8 cm
2	5	
3		16 cm
4		

3. Answer the questions about the patterns.
    (a) How many squares are there in pattern 15?
    (b) What is the length of the perimeter of pattern 25?
    (c) Which pattern number contains 39 squares?
    (d) Which pattern number has a perimeter of 144 centimetres?

Did you know?

Look at this pattern:

12 345 679 × 9 = 111 111 111

12 345 679 × 18 = 222 222 222

12 345 679 × 27 = 333 333 333

12 345 679 × 36 = 444 444 444

12 345 679 × 45 = 555 555 555

What do you think the next four calculations in the sequence are?

Chapter 18: Rotation

Rotation means to move like a wheel. The hour hand of a clock rotates.

Between 12 o'clock and 3 o'clock it rotates through 90° (1 right angle or a $\frac{1}{4}$ turn).

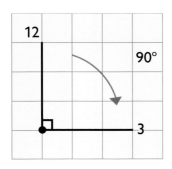

Between 12 o'clock and 6 o'clock it rotates through 180° (2 right angles or a $\frac{1}{2}$ turn).

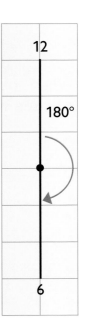

Between 12 o'clock and 9 o'clock it rotates through 270° (3 right angles or a $\frac{3}{4}$ turn).

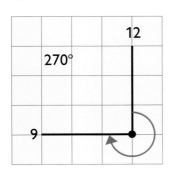

Between 12 o'clock and 12 o'clock it rotates through 360° (4 right angles or 1 complete turn).

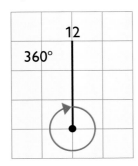

The rotations on the previous page have been made in a **clockwise** direction. This is the same direction as the hands of a clock turn. However, you can rotate a line in the opposite direction which is called **anti-clockwise**.

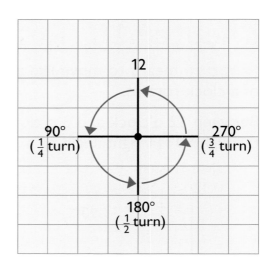

Rotating a line

When rotating a line, it can help to cover the line with your pencil and rotate it to see where it ends up. The **centre of rotation** is often labelled P.

Examples:

(i) Rotate the line through 90° clockwise about P.

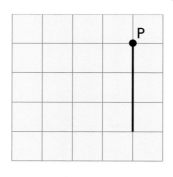

Steps:

- Find the centre of rotation.
- Cover the line with your pencil as you did when drawing angles.
- Then make sure you know in which direction you are rotating the line: clockwise in this example.
- Rotate through the angle and then draw the new line.

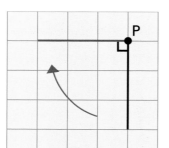

(ii)   Rotate the line through 180° about P.

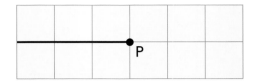

Rotate your pencil first, then draw the line.
Note: 180° is a half turn which gives the same result whether you rotate the line either clockwise or anti-clockwise.

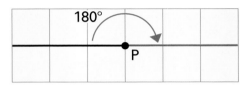

(iii) Rotate the line through 270° anti-clockwise about P.

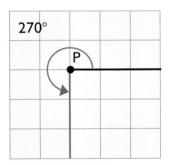

Exercise 18.1: Rotating a line

Copy the grid and draw the rotations.

1.

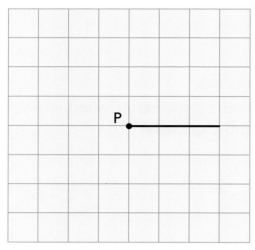

(a) Rotate the line clockwise through 90° about P. Label your line (a).

(b) Rotate the line through 180° about P. Label your line (b).

(c) Rotate the line 90° anti-clockwise about P. Label your line (c).

2.

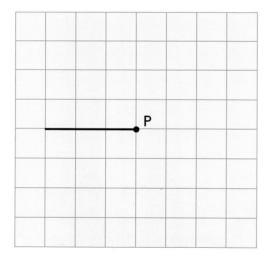

(a) Rotate the line clockwise through 90° about P. Label your line (a).

(b) Rotate the line 90° anti-clockwise about P. Label your line (b).

3.

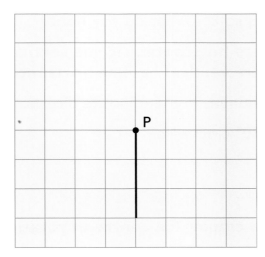

(a) Rotate the line 90° anti-clockwise about P. Label your line (a).

(b) Rotate the line 270° clockwise about P. Label your line (b).

4.

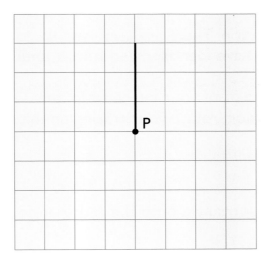

(a) Rotate the line 90° clockwise about P. Label your line (a).

(b) Rotate the line $\frac{1}{2}$ turn about P. Label your line (b).

(c) Rotate the line $\frac{1}{4}$ turn anti-clockwise about P. Label your line (c).

Look back at the rotations you have seen so far. What do you notice?

- After a rotation of 90° lines that were **horizontal** become **vertical**; lines that were **vertical** become **horizontal**.

- After a rotation of 180° the line continues in the opposite direction.

- 270° anti-clockwise is the same as 90° clockwise.

Rotating a shape

We rotate shapes in the same way. In this chapter the **centre of rotation** is always one of the corners of the shape.

To describe a rotation:

- First look for the point where a line meets its image.

- Then work out the angle of the rotation. There are two ways to do this:
  - Put your pencil over the line you have identified and turn it until it covers the image; or
  - Trace the shape; then, using the point of your pencil to fix the tracing paper at the point of rotation, rotate your tracing until it covers the image.

Example:

Describe the rotation that maps the black triangle onto the red triangle.

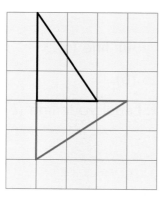

The shortest line and its image meet at point P.

The triangle has been rotated clockwise through 90°.

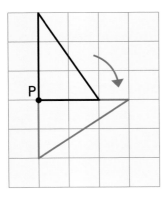

You might also find tracing paper useful when you are asked to rotate a shape yourself.

It is always a good idea to choose one of the lines in the shape and think about what will happen to it when it is rotated.

Example:

Rotate a triangle through 180° about P.

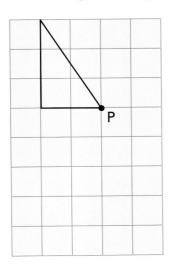

Make a tracing of the triangle.

Look at the base line of the triangle. It is horizontal. After a rotation of 180° it will continue to the right of P.

Fix the tracing paper to the point of rotation with your pencil. Rotate the tracing through 180° (90° twice).

Mark the other two vertices of the image and join them up.

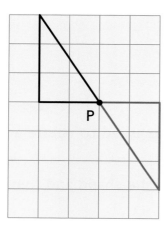

Exercise 18.2: Rotating a shape

1. Describe the rotations that map the black triangles onto the red triangles.

(a)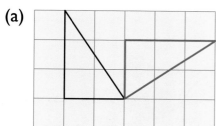

(b)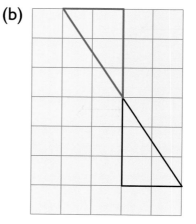

2. Describe the rotations that map the black triangles onto the red triangles.

(a)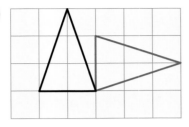

(b)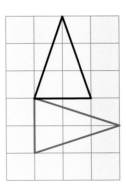

(c)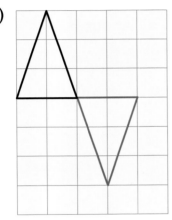

(d)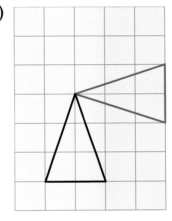

3. (a) Rotate the triangle through 180° about P.

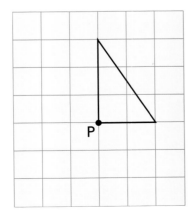

(b) Rotate the triangle clockwise through 90° about P.

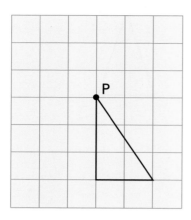

4. (a) Rotate the rectangle clockwise through 90° about P.

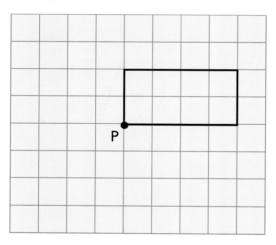

(b) Rotate the rectangle clockwise through 90° about P.

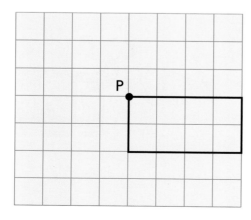

5. Copy the grid and complete the following rotations.

   (a) Rotate the rectangle through 180° about P. Label your rectangle (a).

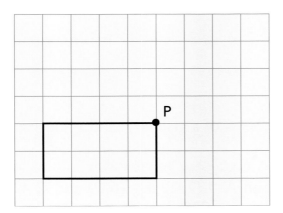

   (b) Rotate the rectangle anti-clockwise through 90° about P. Label your rectangle (b).

6. (a) Rotate the square clockwise through 90° about P.

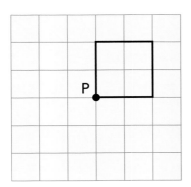

   (b) Rotate the square through 180° about P.

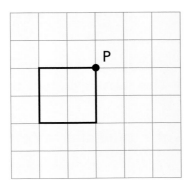

(c) Rotate the square anti-clockwise through 270° about P.

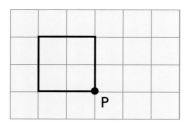

For Q7 and Q8 you will need two copies of a grid with the x and y axes from 0 to 12 (see 📄)

7. (a) (i) Draw triangle ABC when A = (2, 2) B = (6, 2) and C = (6, 4).
        (ii) Rotate triangle ABC through 90° clockwise about C.

    (b) (i) Draw triangle XYZ when X = (8, 10) Y = (7, 7) and Z = (9, 7).
        (ii) What type of triangle is XYZ?
        (iii) Rotate triangle XYZ through 180° about Z.

8. (a) (i) Draw PQRS when P = (1, 7) Q = (1, 12) R = (3, 12) and S = (3, 10).
        (ii) Rotate PQRS through 90° clockwise about P.

    (b) (i) Draw ABCD when A = (10, 6) B = (8, 9) C = (10, 12) and D = (12, 9).
        (ii) What special name is given to ABCD?
        (iii) Rotate ABCD through 180° about A.

Rotational symmetry

Symmetry means that a shape, or part of a shape, **looks the same** after something has been done to it.

You have already learnt that a shape has **line symmetry** if one half of it maps onto the other half (the two halves **look the same**, except that they are mirror images of each other).

A shape has **rotational symmetry** if it looks the same after a certain amount of **rotation**.

Here are some examples that you may recognise:

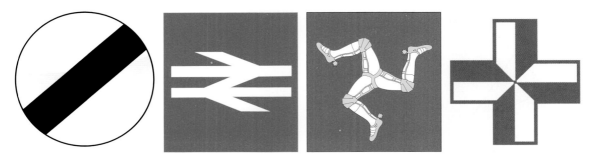

We can use these signs to understand what rotational symmetry is:

- Make a tracing of each shape.
- Put it over the shape and rotate it through a complete rotation.
- Count how many times the tracing maps onto the shape.
- The number you get is the order of rotational symmetry of the shape.

Your answers should be:

| 2 | 2 | 3 | 4 |

Note: If you rotate a shape and the answer is 1, then the shape has **no rotational symmetry**.

Exercise 18.3: Rotational symmetry

1. Copy and complete the table to show the rotational symmetry of the different shapes.

   It might help you to draw the shapes.

Shape	Order of symmetry
Scalene triangle	
Isosceles triangle	
Equilateral triangle	
Rectangle	
Parallelogram	
Square	

Shape	Order of symmetry
Rhombus	
Regular pentagon	
Regular hexagon	

2. A regular figure is one that has all sides and angles equal.

    (a) Which of the shapes in the table above are regular?

    (b) What is the connection between the number of sides of a regular figure and its order of rotational symmetry?

    (c) What do you think is the order of rotational symmetry of
        (i)   a regular decagon?
        (ii) a regular 20-sided figure?

End of chapter activity: Find the numbers

A, B and C represent three different numbers.

You are given the total of two columns and 1 row.

	C	A	B	C	
	B	A	A	B	
	B	A	B	C	
	C	A	C	A	22
		20	17		

Work out the value of each letter and the missing totals.

Did you know?

Your brain is divided into two sides. The left side of your brain controls the right side of your body; and, the right side of your brain controls the left side of your body.

Chapter 19: Area and perimeter

Area of a rectangle

You already know that **area** means how much surface is covered by a shape.

It is measured in **square units**. The most common are:

- the square centimetre (cm²)
- the square metre (m²).

We can find the area of a **rectangle** by counting the number of centimetre squares.

Example:

The area is 24 cm². Count the boxes – each one is 1 cm²

However, not all shapes are drawn accurately on centimetre squared paper. We need a method which will work for **all** rectangles.

Let's have another look at the rectangle above.

- There are 6 centimetre squares along the length.
- There are 4 centimetres along the width (also called the breadth).
- To find the area quickly, multiply 6 by 4 to give 24

This shows us that we can find the area of a rectangle by multiplying the length and the width together.

We can write this as a formula:

Area of a rectangle = length (*l*) × width (*w*)

Example:

What is the area of the rectangle?

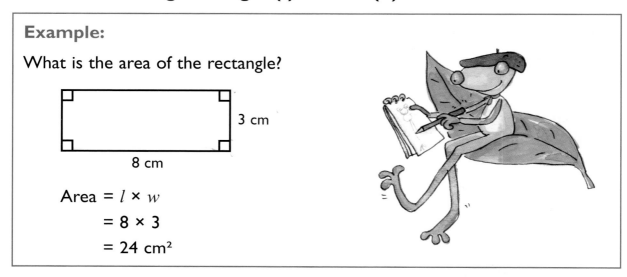

3 cm

8 cm

Area = *l* × *w*

    = 8 × 3

    = 24 cm²

If you are just given the dimensions of the rectangle, it is a good idea to sketch it first.

Example:

Calculate the area of a rectangle that is 7.5 cm long and 5 cm wide.

First sketch the rectangle.

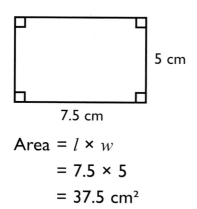

5 cm

7.5 cm

Area = *l* × *w*

    = 7.5 × 5

    = 37.5 cm²

Always remember to include the correct units in your answer.

Exercise 19.1: Area of a rectangle

1. Find the area of each of the following rectangles:

(a)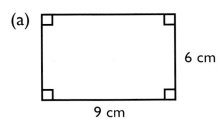

6 cm

9 cm

(c)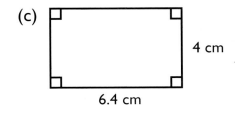

4 cm

6.4 cm

(b)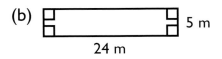

5 m

24 m

2. Calculate the area of rectangles with the following measurements:

	Length	Width
(a)	7 cm	5 cm
(b)	12 cm	9 cm
(c)	15 m	4 m
(d)	50 cm	6 cm
(e)	36 m	8 m
(f)	4.3 m	2 m
(g)	5.8 m	3 m
(h)	9.5 cm	6 cm
(i)	12.3 cm	10 cm
(j)	20 cm	0.5 cm

Finding the length and width of a rectangle

You know that the **factors** of a number make that number when multiplied together. You also know that division is the **inverse** of multiplication. So you know that there are three calculations associated with every factor pair.

Example:

$$48 = 6 \times 8$$

So $\qquad 48 \div 6 = 8$ or $\frac{48}{6} = 8$

and $\qquad 48 \div 8 = 6$ or $\frac{48}{6} = 6$

It follows that if **area = length × width** ($A = l \times w$)

then **length = area ÷ width** ($l = A \div w$) or $\frac{\text{area}}{\text{width}}$ ($l = \frac{A}{w}$)

and **width = area ÷ length** ($w = A \div l$) or $\frac{\text{area}}{\text{length}}$ ($w = \frac{A}{l}$)

Examples:

(i) What is the width of a rectangle which is 10 cm long and has an area of 30 cm²?

Again, you might find a sketch helpful.

Area = 30 cm²

10 cm

$w = A \div l$

$\quad = 30 \div 10$

$\quad = 3$ cm

(ii) What is the length of a rectangle which has an area of 56 m² and is 4 m wide?

Area = 56 m²　　　　　　4 m

$l = A \div w$

$= 56 \div 4$

$= 14$ m

Exercise 19.2: Finding the length and width of a rectangle

1. Calculate the widths of the following rectangles:

	Area	Length
(a)	18 m²	6 m
(b)	72 cm²	12 cm
(c)	63 m²	9 m
(d)	56 cm²	8 cm
(e)	100 cm²	25 cm

2. Calculate the lengths of the following rectangles:

	Area	Width
(a)	28 m²	4 m
(b)	87 m²	3 m
(c)	125 m²	5 m
(d)	144 cm²	8 cm
(e)	222 cm²	6 cm

Composite shapes

To find the area of a composite shape:

● First divide the shape into separate rectangles.

● Then find the area of each rectangle.

● Add all the areas together.

Sometimes you will need to work out the length or width of some of the rectangles before you can calculate the areas. Use the lengths of any parallel lines to help you.

Examples:

(i) Calculate the area of the shape below. (All measurements are in centimetres)

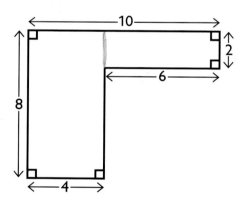

Split the shape into two rectangles (there are two ways you can do this), then calculate the areas separately and add them together.

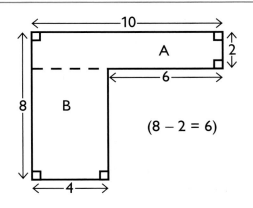

Area A = l × w or   Area A = l × w

         = 8 × 4   = 10 × 2

         = 32 cm²   = 20 cm²

Area B = l × w Area B = l × w

         = 6 × 2   = 6 × 4   (length = 8 − 2)

         = 12 cm²   = 24 cm²

A + B = 32 + 12   A + B = 20 + 24

         = 44 cm²   = 44 cm²

(ii)   Calculate the area of the shape below. (All measurements are in metres.)

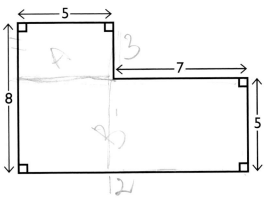

Split the shape into two rectangles (there are two ways you can do this), then calculate the areas separately and add them together.

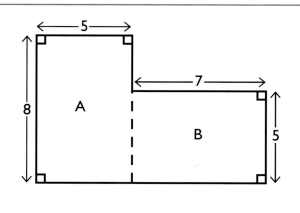

Area A = $l \times w$ or   Area A = $l \times w$

       = 8 × 5   = 5 × 3   (width = 8 − 5)

       = 40 m²   = 15 m²

Area B = $l \times w$ Area B = $l \times w$

       = 7 × 5   = 12 × 5   (length = 5 + 7)

       = 35 m²   = 60 m²

A + B = 40 + 35   A + B = 15 + 60

       = 75 m²   = 75 m²

Exercise 19.3: Composite shapes

Calculate the area of each of the following shapes.

Q1–3: All measurements are in centimetres.

1.

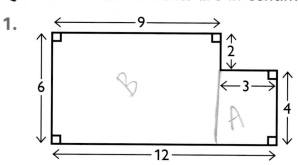

2.

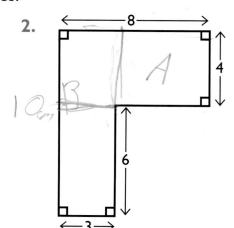

3.

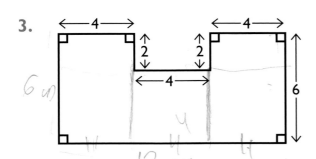

6 m

12 cm

3×5=15
10×4=40
55

Q 4–6: All measurements are in metres.

4.

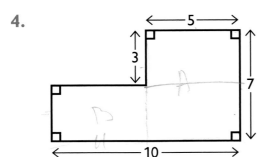

A = 5×7 = 35
B = 5×4 = 20
55

5.

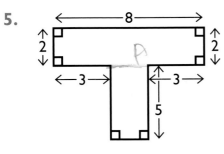

A = 2×8 = 16
B = 5×2 = 10
26
A+B = 26

6.

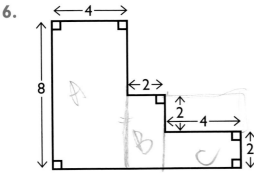

A = 8×4 = 32
B = 2×4 = 8
C = 2×4 = 8
48

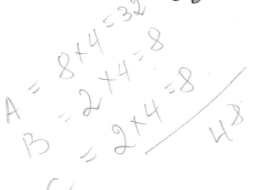

Area of a square

A **square** has equal length and width.

We can use the formula for finding the area of a rectangle to find the area of a square:

Area = l × w

Because, in a square, l = w, we can write this as:

Area of a square = l × l or Area = l^2

Example:

What is the area of a 5 cm square?

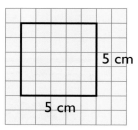

5 cm

5 cm

Area = l × l

       = 5 × 5

       = 25 cm²

Exercise 19.4: Area of a square

Find the areas of squares with these side lengths:

1. 3 m

2. 7 cm

3. 9 m

4. 11 cm

5. 20 cm

Finding the side length of a square

To find the **side length** of a square you need to find that factor which, when multiplied by itself, produces the area.

Remember: A square root is the **inverse** of a square number.

The side length of a square is the square root of the area:

Area = length × length ($A = l^2$)

length = √Area ($l = \sqrt{A}$)

Example:

What is the side length of a square whose area is 36 cm²?

$$l = \sqrt{A}$$
$$= \sqrt{36}$$
$$= 6 \text{ cm}$$

Exercise 19.5: Finding the side length of a square

Find the side lengths of squares with these areas:

1. 16 cm²

2. 64 m²

3. 4 m²

4. 1 m²

5. 100 cm²

Area of a right-angled triangle

A **right-angled triangle** is half a rectangle or half a square.

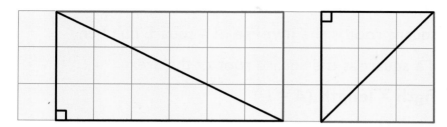

The area is **half** the area of the completed rectangle or square. So we can find the area of a right-angled triangle by finding the area of the related rectangle or square and dividing it by 2

This gives us the formula:

Area of a right-angled triangle = $\frac{1}{2} \times l \times w$ or $(l \times w) \div 2$

Examples:

(i) Find the area of this right-angled triangle.

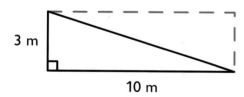

3 m

10 m

$$\text{Area} = \frac{1}{2} \times l \times w$$
$$= \frac{1}{2} \times 10 \times 3$$
$$= 15 \text{ m}^2$$

(ii) Find the area of this right-angled triangle.

5 cm

5 cm

$$\text{Area} = \frac{1}{2} \times l \times l$$
$$= \frac{1}{2} \times 5 \times 5$$
$$= 12\frac{1}{2} \text{ cm}^2 \text{ (or 12.5 cm}^2\text{)}$$

Exercise 19.6: Area of a right-angled triangle

Find the area of each of these right-angled triangles:

1.

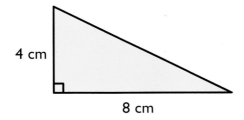

4 cm

8 cm

2.

5 cm

12 cm

3.

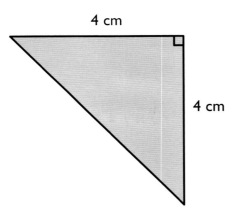

4 cm

4 cm

4.

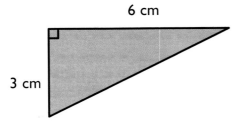

6 cm

3 cm

5.

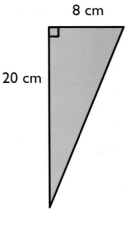

8 cm

20 cm

6.

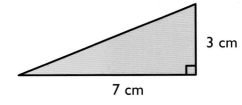

3 cm

7 cm

7.

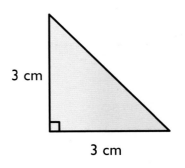

3 cm

3 cm

8.

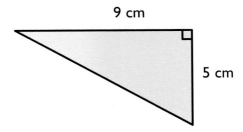

9 cm

5 cm

9.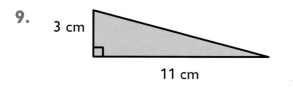

3 cm

11 cm

10.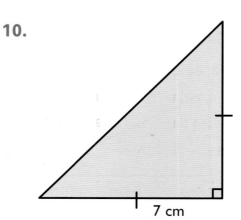

7 cm

Perimeter

Perimeter means the distance round a shape.

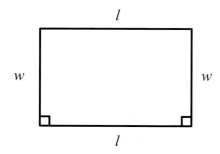

l

w w

l

Perimeter of a rectangle $= l + w + l + w$

$$= 2l + 2w \quad \text{or} \quad 2(l + w)$$

In a square, $l = w$, so

Perimeter of a square $= 4l$

As for area calculations, it might help you to draw a sketch when working with perimeter.

Exercise 19.7: Perimeter

1. Calculate the perimeters of rectangles with these measurements:
   (a) length = 7 cm and width = 3 cm
   (b) length = 5.5 m and width = 4 m

2. What is the length of the perimeter of a 25 cm square?

3. A rectangle has a perimeter of 30 cm. What is its width if it is 10 cm long?

Summary

- Area of a rectangle = $l \times w$

  length = $A \div w$

  width = $A \div l$

- Perimeter of a rectangle = $2(l + w)$

- Area of a square = l^2

  side length = $\sqrt{A}$

- Perimeter of a square = $4l$

- Area of a right-angled triangle = $\frac{1}{2} \times l \times w$

Exercise 19.8: Summary exercise

1. Calculate the areas of rectangles with these measurements:
   (a) length 9 cm and width 4 cm
   (b) length 8.4 m and width 6 m

2. What is the area of a 7 cm square?

3. Calculate the perimeter of a rectangle with length = 6.7 cm and width = 4.3 cm.

4. How wide is a rectangle which is 12 m long and has an area of 48 m²?

5. What is the length of a rectangle whose area is 120 m² and which is 5 m wide?

6. What is the side length of a square whose area is 9 m²?

7. What is the length of a rectangle which is 8 m wide and has a perimeter of 60 m?

8. The perimeter of a square is 20 cm.

    (a) How long is one side of the square?

    (b) What is the area of the square?

9. Calculate the areas of the following shapes:

    All measurements are in centimetres.

    (a)

    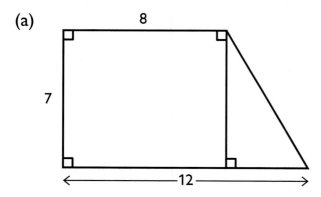

    (b)

    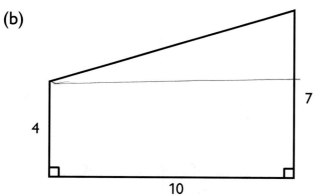

(c)

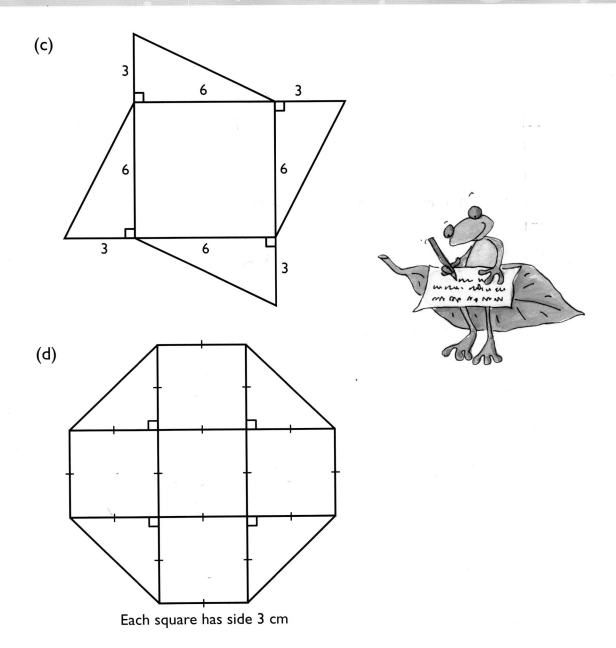

(d)

Each square has side 3 cm

10. There is a square whose area and perimeter have the same value.
What is the length of a side of this square?
(The answer is less than 10 cm.)

Exercise 19.9: Problem solving

1. A postcard measures 15 centimetres by 10 centimetres.
   (a) What is its area?
   (b) What is the length of its perimeter?

   Squares of side 2 centimetres are cut from each corner.

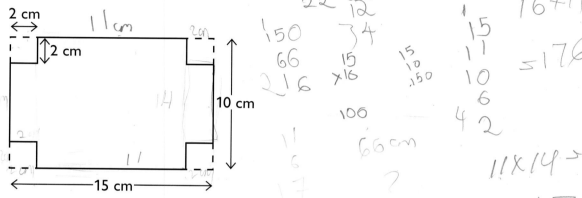

   (c) What is the area of all four squares?
   (d) What area of the original card remains?
   (e) What is the length of the new perimeter?

2. Dr Quack's consulting room is rectangular, measuring 5 metres by 4 metres.

   (a) What is the area of the room?

   He covers the whole floor with carpet which costs £35 per m².

   (b) What is the cost of the carpet?

3. Peter's lawn is a rectangle which measures 20 metres by 16 metres.
   (a) What is the area of the lawn?

   A packet of weed killer, which costs £1.32, is enough to cover 30 m².

   (b) How many packets must he buy to cover the lawn and what will they cost?

4. Beatrix McGregor has a vegetable patch in the shape of a rectangle. It measures 15 metres by 8 metres.

(a) What is the area of the patch?

In one corner there is a shed which measures 3.5 metres by 2 metres as shown in the diagram.

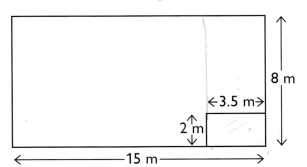

(b) What is the area of the shed floor?

40 square metres are taken by paths and the compost heap.

(c) What area remains for Beatrix to grow vegetables?

She wants to surround her total patch with wire.

(d) How many metres of wire will she use?

5. The diagram shows the field where Billy keeps a pair of goats.

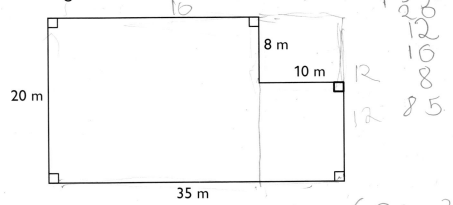

(a) What area do the goats have to graze?

(b) What is the perimeter of the field?

6. The school photograph, which measures 52 centimetres by 20 centimetres, is mounted on white card and then framed as shown in the diagram.

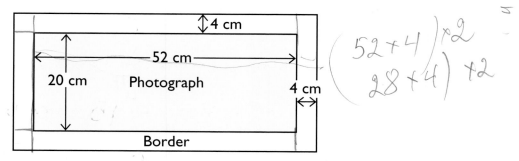

The white border is 4 centimetres wide all the way round.

(a) What is the total length of picture frame that is needed?

(b) What is the area of the white border?

7. A groundsman wants to put rope around the edge of the school cricket square. The square is 9 metres wide and has an area of 216 square metres. How much rope does he need?

8. David's patio is a rectangle which measures 8 metres by 5 metres. He paves it with slabs which are 50 centimetre squares.

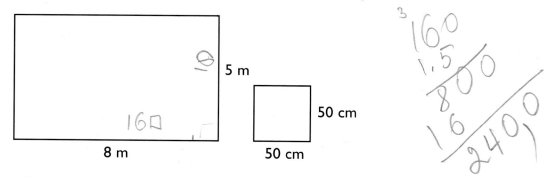

(a) How many slabs can he fit along the length of the patio?

(b) How many slabs can he fit along the width of the patio?

(c) How many slabs must he buy to pave the whole patio?

Slabs cost £1.50 each.

(d) How much will David pay for all the slabs?

End of chapter activity: A range of rectangles

A rectangle has length and width which are a whole number of metres.

1. If the perimeter is 20 metres long, write down all the possible measurements and the corresponding areas.

   *[handwritten: 25cm² 21m² 24m² 16m² 9m²
   (5,5,5) (7,3)(6,4) (8,2)(1,9)]*

2. If the area is 20 metres², write down all the possible measurements and the corresponding perimeters.

   *[handwritten: 10x2 1x20 5x4
   (P24) (P42) (P18)]*

3. John has a rope that is 100 metres long. What is the largest area that John can enclose inside a rectangle?

   *[handwritten: Perimeter! 20,20,30,30 Perimeter! 25,25,25,25
   600 Area   625 Area]*

4. Keith is going to rent a rectangular plot of land which has an area of 100 metres² from a farmer. He wants a plot with the largest possible perimeter. What dimensions should Keith ask the farmer for and how much rope will he need to enclose the plot?

Did you know?

Paper sizes are found by halving.

The largest size is called size 0 and measures 841 mm by 1189 mm.

This is folded in half across the longest side and then rotated through 90° to give size 1

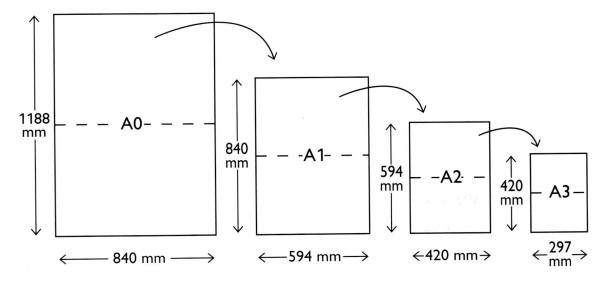

This process is repeated until size 10

Sizes (in mm):

A0	840 × 1188	
A1	594 × 840	
A2	420 × 594	
A3	297 × 420	
A4	210 × 297	(This is the most common size.)
A5	148 × 210	
A6	105 × 148	
A7	74 × 105	
A8	52 × 74	
A9	37 × 52	
A10	26 × 37	

Chapter 20: 3D shapes

You should already be familiar with many of the most common **three-dimensional (3D)** shapes.

Remember, each 3D shape has:

- **faces** which are 2D (plane) shapes;
- **edges** which are straight lines where the faces meet;
- **vertices** (corners) which are points where the edges meet.

Nets

To make a model of a 3D shape, you draw its **net** (flattened shape) on paper in two dimensions.

Cube

A **cube** is a 3D shape with six square faces which are all the same size

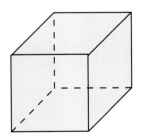

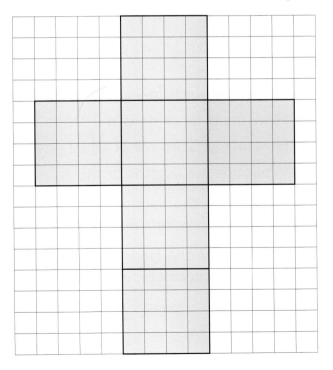

Here is the net of this cube:

Cuboid

A **cuboid** is a rectangular box with six rectangular faces.

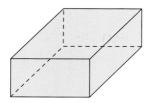 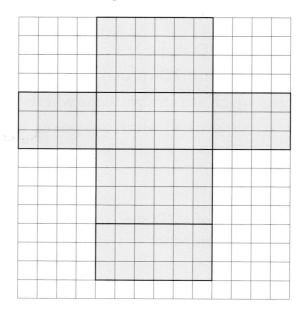

Here is the net of this cuboid:

Exercise 20.1: Nets of cubes and cuboids

1. Collect some cardboard boxes (e.g. cereal boxes) and flatten them out to make their nets.

   Answer these questions about each of the nets:

   (a) How many faces does the shape have?

   (b) How many faces are of equal size?

   (c) What are the lengths of the sides of the faces?

2. Copy and draw the nets on page 269 and above, cut them out and fold them along the lines to make a cube and a cuboid.

3. Other nets have the faces arranged in a different way. See if you can draw two different nets for:

   (a) a cube; and

   (b) a cuboid.

Surface area

All the faces of a cube or cuboid are either rectangles or squares. This means that it is easy to work out the **surface area** of the cube or cuboid.

A shape's net shows us the area of all its faces. This is called the **total surface area**.

Cube

All six faces of a cube are squares with the same measurements.

The area of one square can be calculated by multiplying the length of one side by the length of another side.

We can then find the total surface area by multiplying the area of one square by 6

Example:

Find the surface area of a cube with edges of 3 cm each.

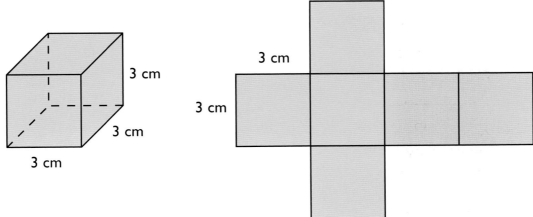

Area of 1 square = 3 cm × 3 cm

$\qquad$ = 9 cm²

Total surface area = 6 × the area of 1 square

$\qquad$ = 6 × 9

$\qquad$ = 54 cm²

Cuboid

A cuboid has three pairs of equal faces:

- top and bottom
- front and back
- the two ends

To work out the total surface area of a cuboid we must first work out the area of one face from each pair. Then we:

- multiply each area by 2 and add the results together; or
- add the areas together and multiply the result by 2

Example:

Find the surface area of this cuboid.

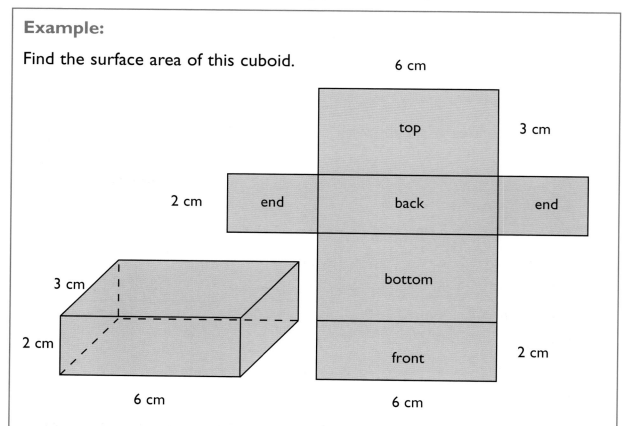

First identify the pairs of faces and find the area of one face from each pair:

- top and bottom (each measure 6 cm × 3 cm) Area is 6 × 3 = **18** cm²
- front and back   (each measure 6 cm × 2 cm) Area is 6 × 2 = **12** cm²
- both ends   (each measure 3 cm × 2 cm) Area is 3 × 2 = **6** cm²

Now work out the total surface area:

Method 1:

(2 × area of top) + (2 × area of front) + (2 × area of end)

= (2 × **18**) + (2 × **12**) + (2 × **6**)

= 36 + 24 + 12

= 72 cm²

Method 2:

= 2 × [(area of top) + (area of front) + (area of end)]

= 2 × [**18** + **12** + **6**]

= 2 × 36

= 72 cm²

Exercise 20.2: Area with cubes and cuboids

1. (a) On centimetre squared paper draw accurately the net of a 4 centimetre cube.

   (b) Calculate the total surface area of the cube.

2. (a) How many faces does a cube have?

   (b) What is the area of one face of an 8 centimetre cube?

   (c) What is the total surface area of the cube?

3. The total surface area of a cube is 600 cm².

   (a) What is the area of one face of the cube?

   (b) What is the length of a side of the cube?

4. A cuboid is 6 centimetres long, 4 centimetres wide and 2 centimetres high.

   (a) On centimetre squared paper draw accurately the net of the cuboid.

   (b) Calculate the total surface area of the cuboid.

5. Below is the net of an open cube with the base shaded. (An open cube has five faces – it does not have a 'lid'.)

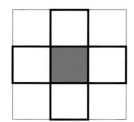

Which of the following are also nets of open cubes? (It may help to copy them and cut them out.)

(a)

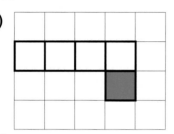

(e)

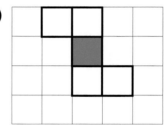

(b)

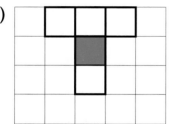

(f)

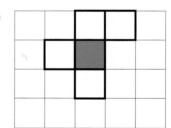

(c)

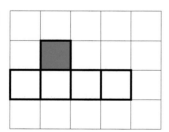

(g)

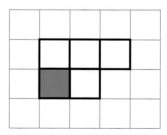

(d)

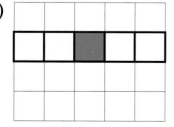

(h)

(i)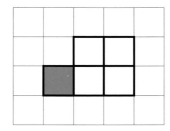

(j)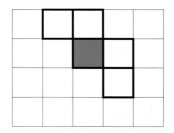

6. Which of the following are nets of cuboids?

(a)

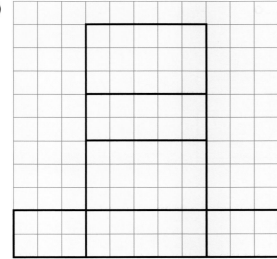

(b)

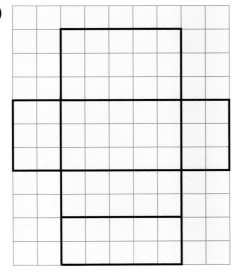

(c)

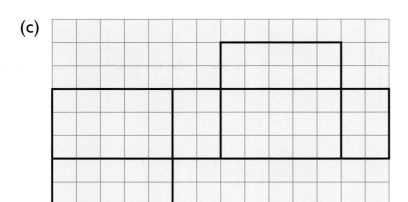

(d)

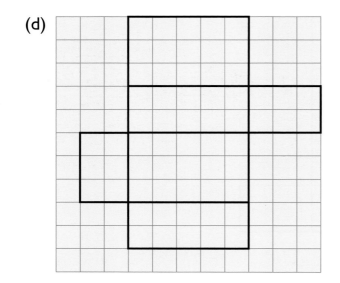

Other nets

You may like to copy these nets to make models of the solid shapes.

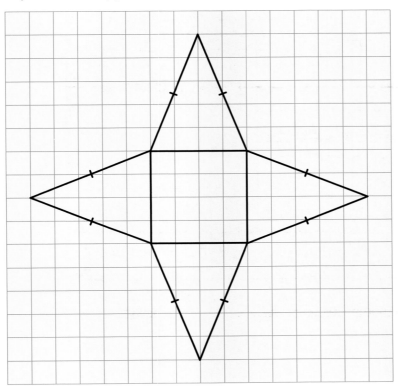

Net of a square-based pyramid

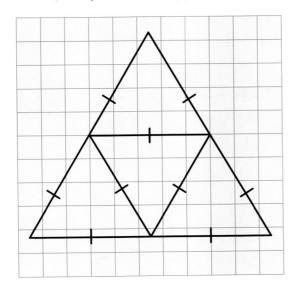

Net of a tetrahedron

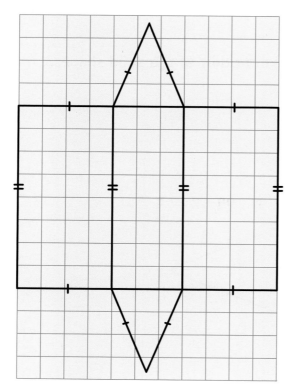

Net of a triangular prism

Volume

Volume is the amount of **space** a shape occupies.

It is measured in **cubic units**, for example the **cubic centimetre (cm³)**.

1 cm³ is the space occupied by a cube that measures 1 cm by 1 cm by 1 cm.

Cuboid

(i)   This cuboid is 5 cm long, 3 cm wide and 1 cm high.

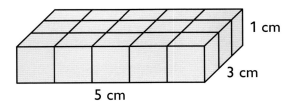

It is made of 1 layer of 5 × 3 = 15 centimetre cubes.

1 × 15 = 15 so the volume is 15 cm³.

(ii) This cuboid is 5 cm long, 3 cm wide and 2 cm high.

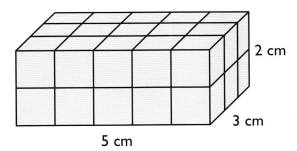

It is made up of 2 layers of 15 centimetre cubes.

You know there are 15 cm³ in 1 layer so the volume is 15 × 2 = 30 cm³

(iii) This cuboid is 5 cm long, 3 cm wide and 3 cm high.

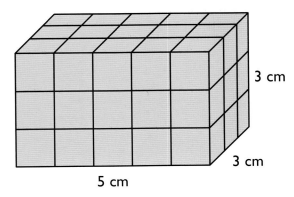

It is made up of 3 layers of 15 centimetre cubes.

The volume is 15 × 3 = 45 cm³

If you look at the cuboids on the previous page you can see that, to find the volume of a cuboid, we:

- multiply **length (l)** by **width (w)** to find the number of cubes in one layer
- multiply the number of cubes in one layer by the number of layers, which is the same as the **height (h)**

This gives us the formula:

Volume of a cuboid = length × width × height or l × w × h

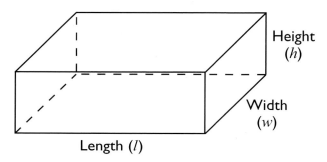

Height (h)

Width (w)

Length (l)

Cube

We can use the same formula to calculate the volume of a cube.

Example:

Find the volume of this cube.

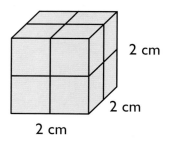

2 cm

2 cm

2 cm

Volume = $l \times w \times h$

$\quad\quad\quad = 2 \times 2 \times 2$

$\quad\quad\quad = 8 \text{ cm}^3$

Exercise 20.3: Volume

1. Calculate the volumes of cuboids with these measurements:

	Length	Width	Height
(a)	5 cm	4 cm	3 cm
(b)	6 cm	5 cm	2 cm
(c)	8 cm	7 cm	5 cm
(d)	10 cm	8 cm	8 cm
(e)	20 cm	10 cm	4 cm

2. Calculate the volumes of cubes with these side lengths:

(a) 4 cm

(b) 5 cm

(c) 10 cm

3. How many cm³ are there in the following shapes?

(a)

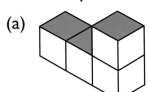

(d)

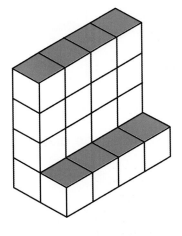

(b)

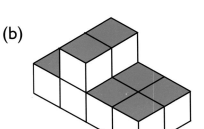

(c)

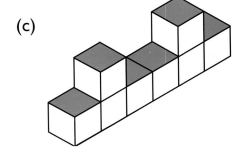

4. Look at the diagram.

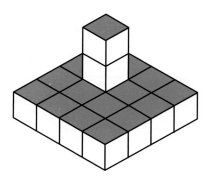

How many cubes are needed to complete a 6 × 3 × 3 cuboid?

5. Look at the diagram.

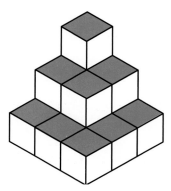

How many cubes are needed to complete a 5 × 3 × 4 cuboid?

6. Look at the diagram.

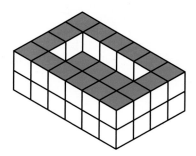

How many extra cubes are needed to make a 5 by 3 by 3 cuboid?

Exercise 20.4: Problem solving

Note: 1 litre has a volume equal to 1000 cm³.

1. Ginger's biscuit tin measures 20 centimetres by 15 centimetres by 10 centimetres. What is the volume of the biscuits that the tin can hold **when full?**

2. A cereal packet has a base which is 22 centimetres by 7 centimetres and is 30 centimetres high.

   (a) What is the volume of the packet?

   Only $\frac{3}{4}$ of the packet is filled with cereal.

   (b) What is the volume of cereal in the packet?

3. A small water trough measures 80 centimetres by 40 centimetres by 30 centimetres.

   (a) What is the volume of the trough?

   (b) How many litres of water are needed to fill the trough when it is empty?

4. Honey keeps her sugar in a tin which is 24 centimetres long, 12 centimetres wide and 12 centimetres deep.

   (a) What is the volume of the tin?

   The tin is empty so she buys 3 packets of sugar which measure 10 centimetres by 7 centimetres by 14 centimetres.

   (b) Will the sugar fit into the tin?

5. A cardboard box has a 40 centimetre square base and is 35 centimetres high. What is its capacity? Give your answer in litres.

6. A wooden die is a 3 centimetre cube.

   (a) What is the volume of the die?

   The wood used has a mass of 0.7 grams per cm³.

   (b) What is the mass of a die?

7. Toby has a set of 162 building bricks which are 4 centimetre cubes.

   He keeps them in a box which has a base measuring 36 centimetres by 24 centimetres.

   (a) How many bricks are there in the bottom layer?

   (b) How many layers are there when all the bricks are in the box?

8. The aquarium in the dentist's waiting room is 60 centimetres long and 30 centimetres wide, and is filled to a depth of 25 centimetres.

   How many litres of water are there in the aquarium?

End of chapter activity: Perfect numbers

2500 years ago, the Greek philosopher Pythagoras and his students wrote about a special kind of number, which they called **perfect numbers**.

A number is perfect if all its factors (except the number itself), when added together, make the number.

Example:

The factors of 6 are   1 × 6

2 × 3

1 + 2 + 3 = 6

6 is a perfect number.

---

1.   What is the next perfect number?

2.   Show that **496** is a perfect number.

Did you know?

Your brain is about 1300–1400 cubic centimetres in volume, about the size of a cantaloupe melon and wrinkled like a walnut.

Chapter 21: Line graphs

Quite often we come across situations where data is collected, providing us with information of some kind. For example, you might record the results of a science experiment, or measure the temperature every day for a month. We can look at this information as numbers, but if is often easier to see patterns if we display the data pictorially.

Pictograms and bar charts

If we collect information about different **types** of something, we can use a **pictogram** or **bar chart** to display it. For example, this bar chart shows the types of transport pupils in Class 5A use to come to school.

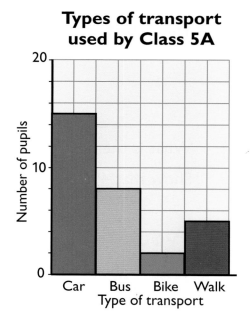

Types of transport used by Class 5A

Line graphs

If the information we collect is a **measurement** (for example, temperature readings, speed during a journey, the rate of growth of a runner bean plant), we can use a line graph.

Example:

Jack recorded his company's sales for one week last October. The figures are in thousands.

Day of the week	Mon	Tues	Wed	Thurs	Fri	Sat	Sun
Sales (£thousands)	3	7	15	10	13	8	1

Draw a graph to show this information.

First draw the axes:

- Put the days of the week along the bottom.
- Put the sales figures up the side. Start at 0 and stop at 16 (it is always a good idea to continue the axis just beyond the largest measurement, in this case 15 (Wednesday)). In the graph below the scale is 1 square to £1000

Then plot the points, one by one:

- Find the day of the week on the horizontal axis, then move up the graph until you are in line with the correct value on the vertical axis.
- Mark the point using a small cross.

Finally, join the points with a line.

Company sales one week last October

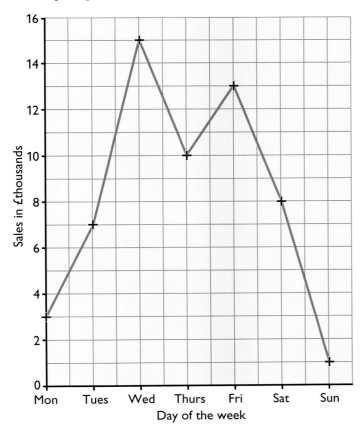

Sometimes you will be asked to use a graph to **estimate** a value. This means that you must read a point off the graph. We use the word **estimate** because we cannot know whether the answer is exact.

When you read points off a graph, you should always check the scale being used on the axes.

Example:

Sue recorded the temperature in degrees centigrade (°C) every 2 hours last Tuesday. Here are her results.

Time	8 am	10 am	Noon	2 pm	4 pm	6 pm
Temperature (degrees centigrade)	13	17	26	30	28	21

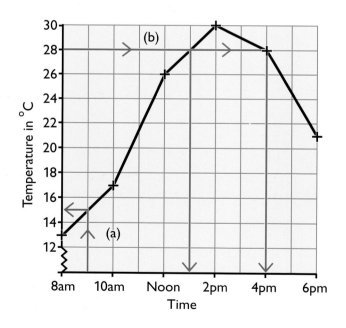

Note: The 'zigzag' at the bottom of the y axis shows that part of the Temperature axis has been left out. The lowest reading is 13 °C so we don't need to show 0−12 °C.

(a)   Estimate the temperature at 9 am.

First check the scales:

- The scale on the x axis is 1 square to 1 hour.
- The scale on the y axis is 1 square to 2 °C.

Now find the value you need to answer the question:

- Find 9 on the Time axis.
- Draw a vertical line, from 9 am, until you meet the graph line.
- Draw a horizontal line, from the graph line, to the Temperature axis.
- Read the value on the Temperature axis. For 9 am it is halfway between 14 and 16, which is 15

The temperature at 9 am was 15 °C.

Note: This is an estimate because we can't be sure that the temperature rose steadily between 8 am and 10 am.

(b)   When was the temperature more than 28 °C?

This time we know the temperature and need to find a time (or times):

- Find 28 on the Temperature axis.
- Draw a horizontal line, from 28 °C, across the graph.
- Find the points where your horizontal line crosses the graph line. At each point, draw a horizontal line down to the Time axis.
- Read the values on the Time axis. They are 1 pm and 4 pm.

The temperature was more than 28 °C between 1 pm and 4 pm.

Note: This is an estimate because we don't know that the temperature was 28 °C at exactly 1 pm. (We *do* know that it was 28 °C at 4 pm.)

Exercise 21.1: Line graphs (1)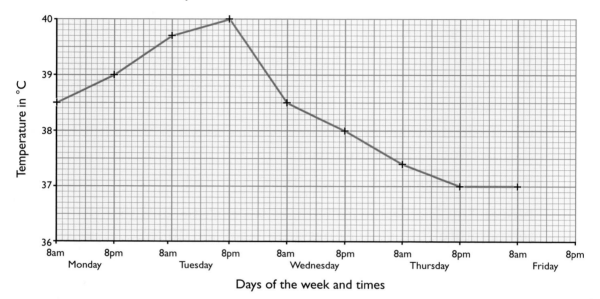

1. Ross is feeling unwell on Monday. His mother finds he has a temperature and tells him to stay in bed. She takes his temperature twice a day and plots the results on a graph.

   Note: A normal temperature is 37°C.

(a) What was Ross's temperature when he was told to stay in bed?

(b) By how much did Ross's temperature rise in the first 24 hours?

(c) What was Ross's highest temperature?

(d) In which 12 hour period did the temperature fall most?

(e) Why do you think there is no record of a temperature at 8 pm on Friday?

2. The graph below shows the monthly rainfall (in mm) in Cairns, Australia.

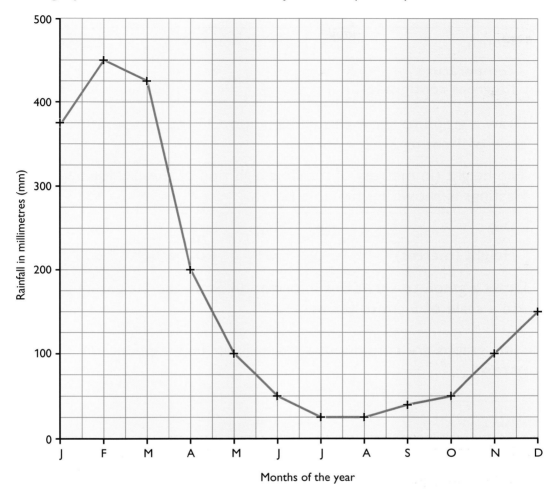

Months of the year

Answer the following questions:

(a) How much rain fell in the wettest month?

(b) Which are the driest months?

(c) How much more rain fell in April than in June?

(d) Can you tell how much rain fell on 15th November?

(e) Why do you think it might be a good idea to give an umbrella as a Christmas present?

3. The average monthly temperature in °C in London is shown in the table below.

Month	Jan	Feb	Mar	Apr	May	Jun	Jul	Aug	Sept	Oct	Nov	Dec
Temperature (degrees centigrade)	4	5	7	9	12	16	18	17	15	11	8	5

Draw a graph to show this information. On the Temperature axis, use a scale of 1 cm to 2 °C.

4. The height (in metres) of the first high tide of the day for a week at Hastings is shown in the table below.

Day	Sun	Mon	Tues	Wed	Thurs	Fri	Sat
Height (metres)	6.9	6.5	6.0	5.9	6.2	6.6	7.0

Draw a graph to show this information. Start the Height axis at 5.5 and use a scale of 5 cm to 0.5 m.

Some line graphs are continuous straight lines. This happens when a change is **constant**.

Example:

Adam fills his empty water butt, which is 90 centimetres deep, with a hosepipe connected to the garden tap. He notices that the water level rises at a rate of 20 cm every 5 minutes.

Plot a graph to show the period it takes to fill the water butt and use it to work out how long it takes to fill completely.

First draw the axes:

- On the Time axis, use a scale of 2 cm to 5 minutes.
- On the Depth axis, use a scale of 2 cm to 20 cm.

Then plot **three** points:

- First plot 0 minutes against 0 cm (the water butt is empty at the start).
- After 5 minutes, the depth of the water has increased by 20 cm, so plot 5 minutes against 20 cm.

● After another 5 minutes (10 minutes in total), the depth of the water has increased by another 20 cm (so is 40 cm deep in total). Plot 10 minutes against 40 cm.

The water level rises at a **constant** rate. This means that we don't have to plot all the points. Instead, we can plot the first three, (0, 0), (5, 20) and (10, 40), and then draw a continuous straight line through them. The line stops at Depth = 90 cm because that is how deep the water butt is. After that it will overflow!

Note: Strictly speaking, you need to plot only two points, but it is a good idea to plot three. That way, it will be obvious if you have made a mistake.

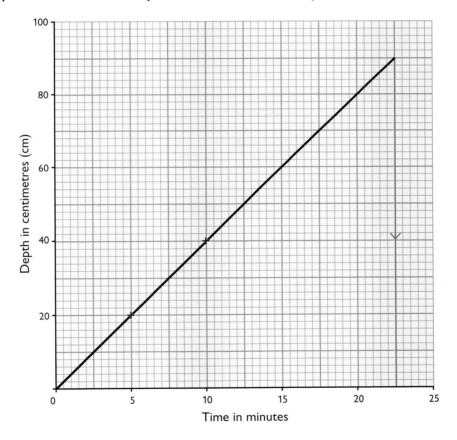

We can then read down from the end of the line to the Time axis, to find how long the butt takes to fill. The answer is halfway between 20 and 25

It takes 22.5 minutes to fill the butt completely.

Exercise 21.2: Line graphs (2)

1. Sally hires a bicycle. She is charged a downpayment followed by an hourly rate. The graph below shows how much a 4 hour hire costs Sally.

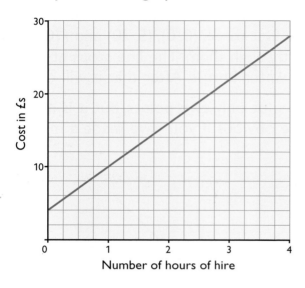

Number of hours of hire

(a) How much does it cost Sally to hire the bicycle for 4 hours?

(b) For how long can a bicycle be hired for £16?

(c) How much must Sally pay for the downpayment?

(d) How much is the hourly rate that Sally is charged?

2. The table below shows some equivalent sums of pounds (£) and euros (€).

Pounds (£)	0	100	200	300	400
Euros (€)	0	125	250	375	500

(a) Use this information to draw a line graph on graph paper, so that you can convert sums up to £400 to euros. Put Pounds on the horizontal axis, using a scale of 2 cm to £100

Put Euros on the vertical axis, using a scale of 4 cm to €100

(b) Use your graph to answer these questions.
    (i) What is the equivalent of €350 in pounds?
    (ii) What is the equivalent of £125 in euros?

End of chapter activity: Two-digit numbers

Hint: You might want to use your calculator for this investigation.

Here are four digits:

   2   3   4   7

1. Using each digit once only list all the possible pairs of two-digit numbers. For example:

    24 and 73

    24 and 37

    and so on.

Before you answer Q2, remind yourself of the meanings of these words:

Sum   The result of adding
Product   The result of multiplying
Difference   The result of subtracting
Quotient   The result of dividing

2. Now look at your list.

    (a) Which pair of numbers gives
        (i) the smallest sum?
        (ii) the largest sum?

    (b) Which pair of numbers gives
        (i) the smallest product?
        (ii) the largest product?

    (c) Which pair of numbers gives
        (i) the smallest difference?
        (ii) the largest difference?

    (d) Which pair of numbers gives
        (i) the smallest quotient?
        (ii) the largest quotient?

Did you know?

If you add up the numbers 1 to 100
(1 + 2 + 3 + 4 + 5 + ... + 100) the total is 5050.

Chapter 22: Arithmetic mean, range, mode and median

Certain types of **data** can be displayed using a **frequency graph**.

Example:

Polly shells 45 peapods and counts how many peas there are in each pod.

She records her results as follows:

5	4	6	3	2	5	6	4	6	5	7	7	5	6	6
4	6	2	6	5	5	7	6	3	2	4	6	4	3	7
4	6	7	5	3	2	3	6	5	4	5	6	4	5	4

She then records the data in a **frequency table**.

Peas	Tally	Frequency
2	IIII	4
3	⑷	5
4	⑸ IIII	9
5	⑸ ⑸	10
6	⑸ ⑸ II	12
7	⑸	5

She then draws a frequency graph.

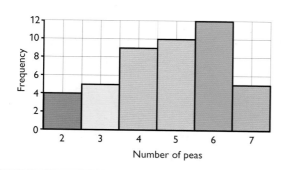

Polly has several questions about the number of peas that can be found in a pod. She wants to know:

- What was the largest number of peas found in one pod?
- What was the smallest number found?
- What is the difference between the largest and the smallest found?
- What is the number of peas most commonly found?
- What was the average number of peas found?
- What was the number of peas in the middle pod?

In this chapter we are going to look at the ways in which we can answer these sorts of questions.

The range

The **range** is the difference between the largest and smallest number of peas in a pod that was recorded.

> **Example:**
>
> By looking at the table or the graph, we can see that the largest number of peas Polly found in a pod was 7 and the smallest number of peas was 2
>
> Range = 7 − 2
>
> $\qquad$ = 5

The mode

The **mode** (adjective is **modal**) refers to the number that appears **most frequently**.

Tip: The words **mode** and **most** both have the same number of letters. Use this fact to help you remember the meaning of **mode**.

> **Example:**
>
> Polly looks at her frequency table and sees that the number of peas with the highest frequency (12) is 6

She looks at her frequency graph and sees that the number of peas with the tallest block is 6

This tells her more peapods had 6 peas in than had any other number of peas.

Mode = 6

Exercise 22.1: The range and the mode

For each of these sets of numbers, write down:

(a) the range; and

(b) the mode.

You might want to use a tally chart to help you.

1.	5	6	4	5	10	3	5	4	9	5	7	9
2.	6	3	1	6	2	3	0	3	4	6	2	6
3.	3	3	1	1	2	1	4	1	4	1	4	4
4.	8	9	7	2	9	8	7	2	7	9	7	8
5.	10	8	12	14	12	10	12	8	12	4	10	8
6.	43	45	49	48	40	41	49	42	46	47	49	44
7.	7.2	8.6	8.5	7.2	8.6	7.3	7.2					
8.	5.6	5.8	5.9	5.6	5.9	5.6	5.7					
9.	1.2	1.8	1.9	1.2	1.8	1.7	1.4	1.3	1.8			
10.	26.2	26.8	26.4	26.7	26.5	26.4	26.6	26.5	26.4			

The median

The **median** is the **middle** number when all the numbers are written in order.

Tip: The words **median** and **middle** both have the same number of letters. Use this fact to help you remember the meaning of **median**.

Example:

Polly wants to find out the median number of peas in a pod.

There are 45 pods altogether so the middle value will be the 23rd.

There are three ways she can find the 23rd value.

Method 1
Polly writes out the number of peas in each pod, starting with the smallest.

Order:	1	2	3	4	5	6	7	8	9	10	11	12	13	14	15
Peas:	2	2	2	2	3	3	3	3	3	4	4	4	4	4	4

Order:	16	17	18	19	20	21	22	**23**
Peas:	4	4	4	5	5	5	5	**5**

Median = 5

Method 2
Polly looks at her frequency table. She adds the numbers in the Frequency column, one at a time.

The first frequency is 4	This tells her that terms 1–4 are 2
4 + 5 = 9	This tells her that terms 5–9 are 3
9 + 9 = 18	This tells her that terms 10–18 are 4
18 + 10 = 28	This tells her that terms 19–28 are 5

Polly now knows that the 23rd term is 5

Median = 5

Method 3
Polly looks at her frequency graph. She adds the heights of the bars, one at a time.

This works the same way as looking at the table.

Median = 5

It was easy to find the middle value because Polly shelled 45 pods.
If the total number of values is an **odd number**, there will always be a middle value.

However, if the total number of values is an **even number**, there will **not** be a middle value. We therefore have to take the mid point between the **two** middle terms.

Example:

A teacher gives a test to ten pupils and marks it out of 20

She wants to find the median mark.

Order:	1	2	3	4	**5**	**6**	7	8	9	10
Marks:	10	13	14	15	**16**	**18**	18	18	19	20

Total number of terms = 10

The median is the mid point between the 5th and 6th terms.

The mid point between 16 and 18 is 17

Median = 17

Exercise 22.2: The median

1. What is the median in each of the following sets of numbers?

   Tip: Write out the numbers in the correct order first.

   (a) 1   2   3   5   7   11   13

   (b) 26   33   39   42   64   87   90

   (c) 13   24   19   13   6   36   17

   (d) 4   18   16   32   9   7   29

   (e) 1.2   3.4   3.2   6.5   9.8   0.4   1.8

   (f) 5   7   11   13   17   19

   (g) 3   6   7   9   10   14   19   21

   (h) 34   46   88   92   104   116   118   144

   (i) 9   12   13   16   20   22   27   31

(j)	34	42	16	85	97	24	18	38
(k)	12	7	9	16	20	7	12	14
(l)	1.2	1.8	1.9	1.6	1.4	1.7	1.4	1.1

2.

AUGUST

						S 1	S 2
						20°	18°
M 3	Tu 4	W 5	Th 6	F 7	S 8	S 9	
17°	18°	17°	21°	21°	19°	18°	
M 10	Tu 11	W 12	Th 13	F 14	S 15	S 16	
18°	19°	24°	26°	26°	27°	27°	
M 17	Tu 18	W 19	Th 20	F 21	S 22	S 23	
29°	30°	29°	28°	30°	26°	26°	
M 24	Tu 25	W 26	Th 27	F 28	S 29	S 30	
25°	24°	23°	24°	20°	19°	19°	
M 31							
18°							

The diagram above shows the midday temperature in degrees Celsius at Salting-on-Sea for each day of August. What was the median temperature for the month?

3.

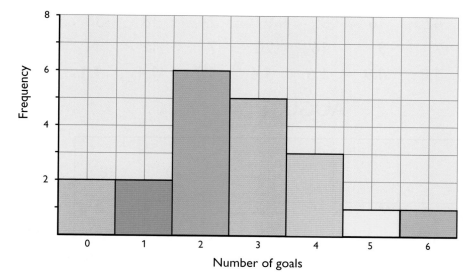

Number of goals

The graph above shows the number of goals scored by the Dribblers Football Club in each of their 20 matches last season. For example, 0 goals were scored on 2 occasions. What was the median number of goals scored?

The mean

The **mean** is the **average** of a set of values. It is the **total** of the values **divided** by the **number** of values.

Mean = $\frac{\text{total of values}}{\text{number of values}}$

Example:

Milly gets the following marks in some tests:

    7   14   18   29

Calculate her mean mark.

Total marks   = 7 + 14 + 18 + 29

                      = 68

Number of marks = 4

Mean   = 68 ÷ 4

                      = 17

If you have a lot of values (like Polly) it is not very easy to add them all up. Instead, you can use your frequency table to help you.

Example:

Polly wants to calculate the mean number of peas in a pod. There are two ways she can do this.

Method 1

Polly looks at her frequency table and sees that:

- 4 pods each contained 2 peas. She writes this as 2 × 4 = 8 peas in total;
- 5 pods each contained 3 peas. She writes this as 3 × 5 = 15 peas in total;
- 9 pods each contained 4 peas. She writes this as 4 × 9 = 36 peas in total;

and so on.

Peas	Frequency	Peas × Frequency
2	4	2 × 4 = 8
3	5	3 × 5 = 15
4	9	4 × 9 = 36
5	10	5 × 10 = 50
6	12	6 × 12 = 72
7	5	7 × 5 = 35
Totals	**45**	**216**

She then adds up the totals and finds that the 45 peapods she shelled contained 216 peas in total.

Mean = 216 ÷ 45

= 4.8

Method 2

Polly looks at her frequency graph. Like the table, it tells her that 4 pods each contained 2 peas, and so on.

Polly does the calculations as before.

Mean = 4.8

Exercise 22.3: The mean

1. Calculate the mean of this set of numbers:

    5   6   4   5   10   3   9   4   9   5

2. What is the mean of this set of numbers?

    23   38   20   30   31   19   27   24   32   26

3. Six people estimate the distance to the church as:

    100 m   130 m   90 m   100 m   150 m   150 m

    Calculate the mean estimate.

4. The masses of five apples are as follows:

    43 g   50 g   46 g   49 g   47 g

    What is the mean mass of the apples?

5. Mary surveyed the cars coming through the school gates and noted down the number of people in each car. Her first 10 results were as follows:

    1   3   1   1   2   4   3   3   1   1

    What is the mean number of people in each car?

6. Barrel Castle's 1st XI scored the following number of goals in each match last season:

    0   3   1   0   2   3   6   3   4   0   2   0

    What was the mean number of goals the team scored?

    Note: The 0 scores must be included in your calculations.

7. Richard buys 10 boxes of matches. He counts the number of matches in each box. His results are as follows:

    48   50   49   51   47   45   43   47   48   52

    What is the mean number of matches in a box?

8. Colin carded the following scores in eight rounds of golf:

    74   70   67   74   78   70   68   75

    What was Colin's mean score for a round?

9. Some children measured the width of their right hands. The results, in centimetres, were:

   6.3   7.1   5.8   6.0   5.5   5.8   6.2   5.3

   What was the mean width of their right hands?

10. Rose compares the price of the same jar of jam in eight different shops. The prices are:

    80p   75p   88p   83p   81p   77p   90p   86p

    What is the mean price of this jar of jam?

11. All members of a group of friends tried to swim as many lengths of a swimming pool as possible in half an hour. The results were as follows:

    4 completed 22 lengths each
    1 completed 19 lengths
    7 completed 17 lengths each
    5 completed 10 lengths each
    3 completed 8 lengths each

    (a) How many friends were there in the group?

    (b) How many lengths altogether did the friends swim?

    (c) What was the mean number of lengths swum by the friends?

12. A collection is made for Mrs Warbick who is leaving at the end of term. Each member of staff gives either a £1 or £2 coin or a £5 or a £10 note. The graph on the next page shows what was donated.

Money donated to Mrs Warbick

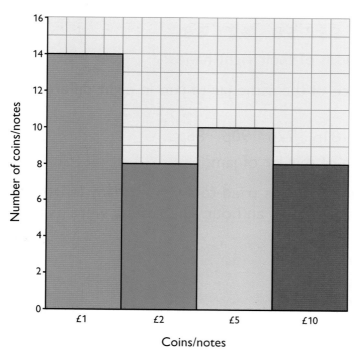

(a) How many members of staff gave to the collection?

(b) How much money was raised altogether for Mrs Warbick?

(c) What was the mean amount of money given by a member of staff?

When you have only two values, the **mean** gives you the **mid point** between those two values. So you can use the same calculation (addition and division) to help you find the **median** when there are two middle values.

Examples:

(i) The mid point of 14 and 18 is 16   (14 + 18 = 32 and 32 ÷ 2 = 16)

(ii) The mid point of 12 and 13 is $12\frac{1}{2}$ (12 + 13 = 25 and 25 ÷ 2 = $12\frac{1}{2}$)

(iii) The mid point of 14 and 19 is $16\frac{1}{2}$ (14 + 19 = 33 and 33 ÷ 2 = $16\frac{1}{2}$)

Summary

The **range** is the difference between the largest and smallest term.

The **mode** is the term that occurs **most** often.

The **median** is the term in the **middle** when all terms are placed in order.

If there is an **odd** number of values, the median is the middle number

If there is an **even** number of terms, the median is the mid point between the middle two terms.

The **mean** (average) is the **total** of all the values **divided** by the **number** of values.

$$\textbf{Mean} = \frac{\text{total of values}}{\text{number of values}}$$

Examples:

(i)   These are the marks gained in a spelling test by Form 5C:

7	4	6	5	7	5	8	7	5	6
9	5	9	7	9	7	6	4	7	5

Tip: It is often helpful to make a frequency table.

Marks	Tally	Frequency	Marks × Frequency
4	II	2	4 × 2 = 8
5	HHT	5	5 × 5 = 25
6	III	3	6 × 3 = 18
7	HHT I	6	7 × 6 = 42
8	I	1	8 × 1 = 8
9	III	3	9 × 3 = 27
Totals		**20**	**128**

(a) What is the range of marks?

Range = 9 − 4   (Largest value minus smallest value)

= 5

(b) What is the modal mark?

Mode = 7   (The mark with the largest frequency)

(c) What is the median mark?

There are 20 values in total, so we need to find the mid point between the 10th and 11th values.

The 10th term is 6 and the 11th term is 7

Median = 6.5   (6 + 7 = 13 and 13 ÷ 2 = 6.5)

(d) What is the mean mark?

Mean = total of all marks divided by the number of marks

= 128 ÷ 20

= 6.4

(ii) The graph shows the ages of the children in the school orchestra.

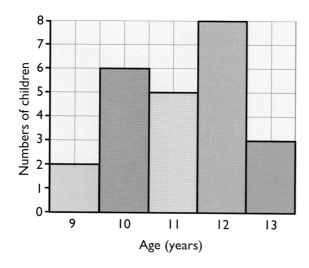

(a) What is the range of ages?

Range $= 13 - 9$ (Largest value minus smallest value)

$= 4$

(b) What is the modal mark?

Mode $= 12$ (The age with the tallest bar)

(c) What is the median age?

There are 24 children in total $(2 + 6 + 5 + 8 + 3)$

The median is the mid point between the 12th and 13th values.

Terms 1–2 are 9

Terms 3–8 are 10

Terms 9–13 are 11

So the 12th and 13th values are both 11

Median $= 11$

(d) What is the mean age?

Total of all the ages $= (9 \times 2) + (10 \times 6) + (11 \times 5) + (12 \times 8) + (13 \times 3)$

$= 268$

Mean $=$ total of all the ages divided by the number of children

$= 268 \div 24$

$= 11\frac{1}{6}$

$= 11$ years 2 months

Exercise 22.4: Problem solving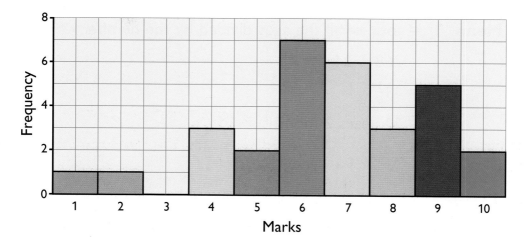

Tip: Draw up a frequency table for each set of results.

1. Luke rolls a die 40 times and records his results as follows:

1	4	3	2	6	1	2	3	4	6
5	5	2	1	4	3	5	6	1	5
3	2	3	3	4	1	5	1	6	1
2	4	5	1	6	2	1	2	5	6

    (a) What is the mode of these results?

    (b) What is the median of these results?

    (c) What is the mean value of these results?

2. Wendy opened her money box to find the following coins:

10p	5p	2p	1p	10p	5p	10p	2p	20p	50p
1p	10p	20p	5p	2p	10p	5p	2p	10p	20p

    (a) What was the range of value of the coins?

    (b) Which value of coin was the modal group?

    (c) What was the median value of the coins?

    (d) What was the mean value of the coins?

3. The graph shows marks gained in a tables test.

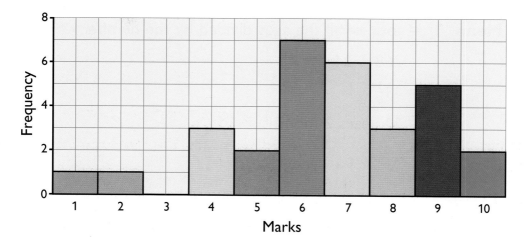

(a) What was the range of marks?

(b) Which mark represents the mode?

(c) What was the median mark?

(d) What was the mean mark?

4.   A group of children are asked how many children there are in their family. Their replies are shown in this graph.

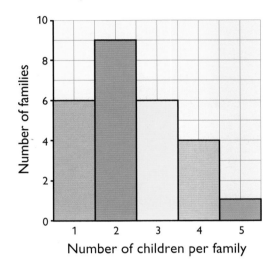

(a) What is the range of the number of children in the families?

(b) What is the modal number of children?

(c) What is the median number of children?

(d) What is the mean number of children per family?

End of chapter activity: Piles of numbers

Peter has the numbers 1 to 10 each written on a separate card.

He wants to divide the cards into two piles so that the numbers in each pile have the same sum when added together.

1.   Explain why Peter cannot do this.

    Hint: What is the 10th triangle number? (See pages 133–134)

2.   What does Peter need to be successful?

Did you know?

The average garden-variety caterpillar has **248** muscles in its head.

Chapter 23: Probability

likely   unlikely   certain   probable   possible   impossible

chance   good chance   poor chance   no chance   even chance

These words can all be used to indicate the **probability** that something will happen.

The probability that something will happen falls between the two measures of:

● the **impossible** – something that won't ever happen (measured at **0**); and

● the **certain** – something will happen (measured at **1**).

We can think of this as a probability scale:

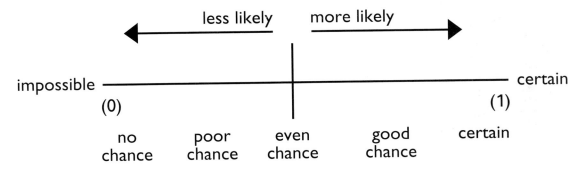

When you decide how likely an event is, you should always be able to explain your reasons.

Examples:

Write in words the probability of each of the following.

(i)   The sun rose in the east this morning.

Certain   (The sun always rises in the east.)

(ii)   You will meet Queen Elizabeth I tomorrow.

Impossible   (Queen Elizabeth I is dead.)

(iii)   Your father will win the Lotto jackpot.

Poor chance/very unlikely   (The chance of winning the Lotto is very small because so many people take part. He might just be very lucky, though!)

(iv)   You will eat potato at lunch today.

Good chance/very likely   (You probably have potatoes quite often at lunch.)

(v)   If a coin is tossed it will show heads.

Even chance   (There are only two faces on a coin, head or tail. If you toss it, it is equally likely that it will land either on its head or on its tail.)

Exercise 23.1: Probability

Write in words the probability of each of the following:

1.   Christmas Day will fall on 25th December.

2.   If today is Friday, tomorrow will be Thursday.

3.   The sun will shine tomorrow.

4.   The driver driving your school bus will be a man.

5.   The card you pick from a full pack will be red.

6.   The next number you throw on a die will be a 6

7.   You will run 100 metres in less than 20 seconds.

8.   The person sitting next to you is a Martian.

9.   You will score more than half marks in your Maths exam.

10.   You will have a holiday abroad next year.

When something happens it is called an **outcome**. Each outcome is separate from another and you cannot predict what the next outcome will be.

For example, if you toss a coin and it comes down heads, this does not affect your next throw. It is still equally likely to land heads as tails.

It is possible for a coin to come down heads seven times in a row. However, the more times you toss a coin, the more likely you are to score an equal number of heads and tails.

Probability is shown by either a fraction or a decimal, between 0 (an impossibility) and 1 (a certainty). It can also be written as a percentage between 0 and 100

The most common way to show a probability is as a fraction in its lowest terms, and that is what we will use in this chapter.

The fraction is worked out as follows:

$$\text{Probability} = \frac{\text{number of successful outcomes}}{\text{number of possible outcomes}}$$

Tip: It is useful to work out the total number of outcomes first.

Example:

A fair die is rolled. This means that there is an even chance of it landing on any one of its faces.

The die has six faces, so there are 6 possible numbers that could occur (1, 2, 3, 4, 5 and 6). That is, the total number of possible outcomes is 6. This is the number that goes on the bottom of the probability fraction.

Now we can look at some questions.

(a) What is the probability of throwing a 4?

There is only 1 successful outcome that meets this criteria (4).

So the probability of throwing a 4 is $\frac{1}{6}$

(b) What is the probability of throwing an even number?

There are 3 even numbers (2, 4 and 6).

So the probability of
throwing an even number $= \frac{3}{6}$

$= \frac{1}{2}$ (Divide top and bottom by 3)

(c) What is the probability of throwing a multiple of 3?

There are 2 multiples of 3 (3 and 6)

So the probability of
throwing a multiple of 3 $= \frac{2}{6}$

$= \frac{1}{3}$ (Divide top and bottom by 2)

Exercise 23.2: Problem solving

1. Write down the first letter of each day of the week. What is the probability of a day of the week starting with the letter T?

2. Write down the first letter of each month of the year. What is the probability of a month of the year starting with the letter M?

3. A box of sweets contains 9 chocolates and 12 toffees. What is the probability that Katy chooses a chocolate?

4.

AEIOU

What is the probability that a vowel has:

(a) a horizontal line of symmetry?

(b) rotational symmetry?

5. Look at the word HIPPOPOTAMUS.

What is the probability of selecting:

(a) the letter S?

(b) the letter P?

(c) a vowel?

6. The numbers 1 to 10 are written on cards which are placed face down on a table.

1   2   3   4   5   6   7   8   9   10

What is the probability that Graham chooses:

(a) the number 7?

(b) an odd number?

(c) a multiple of 4?

(d) a factor of 6?

(e) the number 11?

7.

Using a fair die, what is the probability of throwing:

(a) a 3?

(b) a multiple of 2?

(c) a number that is greater than 3?

(d) a number that is less than or equal to 4?

(e) either a 4 or a 5?

8. Paddy delivers these papers, one to each house:

The Times	6
Daily Mail	9
Daily Express	5
Daily Mirror	10

(a) How many houses are there?

What is the probability that a house, chosen at random, has:

(b) a *Daily Mirror?*

(c) a *Daily Mail* or *The Times?*

(d) neither a *Daily Mail* nor a *Daily Express?*

(e) a *Daily Telegraph?*

9. A set of snooker balls consists of 15 red balls and one each of the following colours: yellow, green, brown, blue, pink, black and white.
What is the probability that Ronnie chooses:

(a) a red ball?

(b) a blue ball?

(c) a black or white ball?

(d) not a yellow or green ball?

10. Linda has a box of hair bands. 4 are yellow, 6 are blue and 8 are green.

(a) What is the probability that she decides to wear:
   (i) a green band?
   (ii) a yellow or blue band?
   (iii) not a yellow band?

Linda puts a yellow band in her hair but loses it at school.

(b) What is the probability that she picks another yellow band from the box next day?

End of chapter activity: Biscuits

A plain biscuit costs 4 pence and a chocolate biscuit costs 9 pence.

Each member of a group of walkers chooses the same number of plain biscuits as each other and the same number of chocolate biscuits as each other.

The total cost is £2.55

How many walkers are there?

Did you know?

A **furlong** is $\frac{1}{8}$ of a mile (220 yards/201 metres).

Originally it was the length of a furrow (say '1 **furrow long**' quickly!) ploughed by a yoke of oxen in a field which was an acre in area.

Today a furlong is used as a distance in horse racing (8 furlongs = 1 mile). The Derby is run over a distance of 1 mile 4 furlongs ($1\frac{1}{2}$ miles).

Chapter 24: Mental strategies

Teacher's introduction

If you used *Junior Maths Book 1* or *Book 2* you will be familiar with the Chapter on Mental Strategies. If you find it necessary to revisit or visit for the first time the various strategies it is available as a free download from the Galore Park website www.galorepark.co.uk

Activity: Logical pets

Five children, Adam, Bella, Connie, Digby and Eve bring their pets to school and ask their class teacher, Mrs Cage to look after them.

The children each own one of the following pets: cat, dog, mouse, parrot or snake.

But who owns which pet?

Use these clues to fill in a copy of the grid and discover who owns which pet:

● Connie and her pet do not start with the same letter.

● Bella's pet has 4 legs.

● Digby owns the snake.

● Adam bought his bird seed from Eve's father who gave his daughter a dog for Christmas.

	cat	dog	mouse	parrot	snake
Adam					
Bella					
Connie					
Digby					
Eve					

Did you know?

The **phonetic alphabet** uses words that can't be confused with anything else to stand for letters of the alphabet. For example, 'B for Bean' could be misheard as 'D for Dean', but 'B for Bravo' doesn't sound like anything else.

If you know the phonetic alphabet, you can make people understand you easily. It is especially helpful on the telephone!

A	Alpha	J	Juliet	S	Sierra
B	Bravo	K	Kilo	T	Tango
C	Charlie	L	Lima	U	Uniform
D	Delta	M	Mike	V	Victor
E	Echo	N	November	W	Whiskey
F	Foxtrot	O	Oscar	X	X-ray
G	Golf	P	Papa	Y	Yankee
H	Hotel	Q	Quebec	Z	Zulu
I	India	R	Romeo		

The post code of GU6 3CD is **Golf Uniform 6 3 Charlie Delta**.

Index